WE WERE THERE AND SURVIVED

By
Matthew T. Fox, Sr.

PUBLISHED BY
HISTORYK PRESS
7 DENDRON COURT
BALTIMORE, MD 21234
visit us on the web at historykpress.com

Copyright © 2005 by Matthew F. Fox, Sr.
All rights reserved
ISBN 978-1-887124-38-6

Printed in the United States of America, 2005

TABLE OF CONTENTS

Introduction	1
Forward	2
Acknowledgements	3
Soldiers and Survivors	5
Credits	99
Appendix	103

INTRODUCTION

Who where the men who fought the battles of the American Civil War? Many of them will never be known, their unidentified photographs often are sold in antique shops and their military records filed in the National Archives or in someone's scrapbook. So often when we think of the Civil War, we think of the great battles fought by legendary generals. Sadly, those who actually fought the war and survived are overlooked. Their stories lost in time, waiting to be told to those who are willing to hear them so they will be passed along to future generations of Americans.

This pivotal period in American history witnessed the deaths of thousands upon thousands of Union and Confederate men alike. It is estimated that two percent of American men were killed during this period. It is quite tragic to think about all the lives lost and what each person must have meant to those waiting back home for their return. They were the fathers, sons, and brothers whose eyes would never meet again with those who had loved them.

Then there are the soldiers who had fought and survived. They too need to be acknowledged for their sacrifices and bravery. Their personal stories and histories will shed better light on what it was like to be an American fighting Americans in the Civil War. This is what I attempt to do in recounting the stories of those who fought and survived.

Foreword

Before the beginning of the American Civil War in 1861 most of America's men lived peacefully on farms, small towns or in cities, they never knew that the next four years would change their lives forever and leave mental and physical scars that would never heal. During the civil war most photographers took pictures of the dead on the battlefield and some of the living whatever was convenient for them too take pictures of none perhaps really shown the faces of those who fought in it the pictures are too blurry or they are too far away to physically see the boys who volunteered to fight for the cause of their country.

I set out to find those veterans that had a story to tell. I wanted to find those who were tucked away and obscured from the public eye to bring them back to life again and have them sit there and spin yarns for us one more time; to learn what it was like to fight against Confederate General Robert E. Lee or Union General Grant. What I found were boys who became men. I also found those who were sent to prisons and survived and those who were maimed and wounded by the instruments of war. During my time compiling these stories I started to feel a part of it seeing the names and the faces of these veterans felt as if I had known them, but that was impossible some have been dead for over 80 to 100 years but still I had that feeling of closeness to them that I want you the reader to feel.

At times I felt the sadness at how most suffered from war time ailments for the rest of their lives and I felt the joy that most lived long and fruitful lives. This will be our monument to the surviving soldiers instead of dedicating a marble and bronze statue for the dead who fell this is a monument to the living for all time for generations to read about their struggle to survive. At first I had no idea where this was going to take me I did not know where to start or begin after hours of searching I found what I was looking for; to me it felt like I discovered a gold mine waiting to be explored. Out of all the soldiers I wanted to include in the book only one family declined my offer to put their relative in the book, it made me sad that he will be forgotten only to remain in their family's mind and not to be shared by others. For the most part other families accepted my offer and gave me all I needed for this project willingly telling me stories about their veteran and sharing everything from their discharge papers to their obituaries. I could tell they wanted their ancestor's story to be known; at one point I was told by one person they did not want their veteran to just sit in a picture frame on a night stand.

This work is an effort not only for me but for the families who gave me the information and pictures. I have spent countless hours putting together this mammoth task of telling their stories at times I fell asleep typing in the wee hours of the morning, was it worth it, the answer is yes, it has been my privilege to bring these men back to life and read their stories and to write about those who were there and survived.

ACKNOWLEDGMENTS

I would like to thank those who have helped me on my long journey to the past with out these people it would not have been possible to even bring this together. I would like to thank Tom Hollowak at Historyk Press for believing in this book. I would also like to thank Tom Ridenour for all the material he has given me. I would further like to thank the following people for whom without them this would not be possible: David J. Huffman, Ryan Beach, Don Parsons, Dr. Harry Sharp, Bea Mansfield, Linda Currie, Elaine Swan, Scot A. Novak, Teri Merchant, Chuck Coulter, Morris Johnson, Martha Henriod, Bob and Linda Thickman, Steve Blackburn, Janet Cornell, Brent Morgan, Larry Rishel, Timothy Adams, Lynn Schneider, Dan and Annette Fay, David White, Richard Temple, Alice Luckhardt, Linda Walls, Michael Grissom, Jean Platt, Arthur Holmes III, William Huber, Bill Lathan, Esther McDermott, Dorothy Smeyers, Elizabeth Grandey, Arlene Baker, Linda Squires, Cheryl and Elroy Christenson, Teri at Oldtime Photos, and I would like to also thank Vonnie Zullo from the horse soldier research service Gettysburg, Pennsylvania. Through my time putting this together I have spent many hours away from my loved ones as well I would like to say thank you to my three wonderful children - Brittany, Matthew, Jr. and Victoria, and to Christina Ghegan for my long absences away from home.

Through out my life the Civil War was a passion beyond belief, I would read about it, watch the movies and even reenact it. I always had a passion for soldier's stories but nothing was really written about them maybe a quote or a chapter but never a full book dedicated to them until now.

I do have to acknowledge a few more people without whom I would not be as knowledgeable about the Civil War: my grandfather Allen Fox, Sr. who is the grandson of my Great-great Grandfather who first planted the seed of the Civil War within me, and to my father who helped me find my families identity; also to my loving mother and step-father who sacrificed vacations to take me to all the battlefields and Civil War attractions in my youth and to help me put a picture to the places I have only read about. I wish also with acknowledge and thank them for all the financial contributions you gave to me to continue doing my hobby. Last but not least, for my brothers - Allen, Ricky, Antonio and Mark thank you for all the love and support you have given me through the years I know it is hard to understand that my passion comes from a war that happened over a hundred years ago, but it is our heritage and remember, to know where you are going in the future you have to know where you were in the past.

To my fellow re-enactors thank you for being the men that you are helping us relive the Civil War so others may know what it was about. Personally I would like to thank Captain Jay Henson and the 7th Maryland Company A re-enactors for welcoming me with open arms into your unit; and to Jeff Bush and Rick Boyle for all the hours we spent on the phone talking about the Civil War and sharing information; and to Colonel Ron Palese for letting me prove myself in the ranks as a officer with the Vincent's Brigade 2nd battalion.

Yes, there were a lot of people who I thanked but I feel without all the support that I have had over the years none of this would be possible. I hope you the reader enjoy this work that has been put together for you to read and share and understand it was written as a group effort from people who have the passion for the Civil War and to keep the memory alive of their loved ones who fought.

SOLDIERS AND SURVIVORS

For the time they all have lived seemed to be ages,
From the time they had fought the battles it was forever!!
For time we were a nation at war it was eternity.

                    Matthew Fox, 2005

ADRONIAN JUDSON ARMAGOST
1848 - 1908

Adronian Judson Armagost was born in Clarion County on March 29, 1848, the son of Rev. I. C. and Elizabeth Stahlman Armagost. When Jud was a boy the family moved to Troy Township where Jud lived until about age 16, then his family moved into Plum Township. When only 16, Jud enlisted in the 112th Pennsylvania Volunteers and fought in seven Civil War battles.

Jud was married to Margaret Jane Grove, who was born in Plum Township on March 25, 1854, the daughter of Grandison W. and Angeline Welsh Grove. They had four children: Lizzie Armagost Dunn, Will Armagost, Nellie Armagost Nelson, and Grant Armagost.

Margaret Jane Grove Armagost died on November 30, 1894. Jud later married Mrs. Carrie Baldensperger, a widow who had three daughters. Jud was in the oil business, and he died of apoplexy in North Clarendon on November 10, 1908.

AdronianArmagost and his second Wife
Mrs.Carrie Baldensperger

BENJAMIN BAXTER
1832 -1885

Benjamin Baxter was born February 9, 1832, in England, the son of Frederick Baxter and Ellen Townsend. Benjamin enlisted twice in the Civil War. He first enlisted on July 5, 1861, in the 14th Massachusetts, Company E, at the age of 27. A weaver from Amesbury, Massachusetts, he was 5' 6", brown hair, blue eyes and light complexion. The regiment was soon changed to the 1st Heavy Artillery. On March 21, 1863, he was medically discharged, due to an injury caused by operating the heavy artillery.

On July 12, 1863, in Webster, Worcester County, Massachusetts, he married Mrs. Grace Robinson Saville, the daughter of William Robinson and Mary Jackson. On December 3, 1863 he re-enlisted in the 2nd Heavy Artillery, Company G. Companies "G" and "H" were assigned to garrison duty at Plymouth, North Carolina. A three day battle soon took place, April 17-20, 1864, that was to change his life forever. On April 20, 1864, after a brave three-day resistance at the Battle of Plymouth, Companies "G" and "H" were made prisoners almost to the man, about 275 being taken into captivity and sent to Andersonville Prison. The Union soldiers became known as the Plymouth Pilgrims.

Benjamin was held prisoner a total of nine months. He was first held a prisoner at Charleston, South Carolina then transferred to Andersonville, near Americus, Georgia until being sent to Florence Stockade in Florence, North Carolina, where he remained until his final parole in December 1864. It took Benjamin two months to return home. He did not appear on hospital records until February 1865.

Everyone thought he died, even Sergeant Warren Lee Goss of Company H, 2nd Massachusetts Heavy Artillery, who wrote of his captivity in, *The Soldier's Story at Andersonville, Belle Isle, and other Rebel Prisons,* [page 245, Lee & Shepard Publishers, Boston, 1866]:

> *Baxter, of Company G, went the same way, though he got his parole, and was on his way North. Shattered in mind and body, he roused himself at the prospect of going home, made the effort, and died. I recollect asking him, at one time, what he thought of southern chivalry. His answer had in it food for thought, which, though it may be indigestible in these lenient times, was the spirit evoked by the barbarous usage of prisoners. "I have made up my mind," said he, "to one creed, political and religious, to govern my conduct when I get out of prison." "What creed is that?" I inquired. "To hate what they love, and love what they hate. I shall be sure, then, to be on the right side.*

William Henry Baxter

He returned to Camp Parole, but the lasting effects of scurvy were responsible for his discharge in August of 1865. After the war Benjamin and Grace, still living in Webster, Massachusetts had one son, William Henry Baxter, born June 18, 1867. They moved to Hancock, Stevens County, Minnesota in the mid 1870s where Benjamin died on May 9, 1885, at the age of 53 and was buried in Lake Side Cemetery. After Benjamin's death Grace moved to Minneapolis about 1890 and lived at 1808 Washington Avenue North.

Truman Beard
1837 - 1903

In the 1860 census Truman Beard is enumerated living with Joel R. Harris, a blacksmith, and his family. Truman is listed as age 21, a blacksmith born in Ohio, Canaan Township in Morrow County.

Truman's muster roll shows him volunteering with the 4th Ohio Volunteer Infantry, organized at Camp Dennison, Ohio on June 4, 1861. The unit moved to Grafton, West Virginia June 20-23, 1861 attached to McCook's advance brigade, and remained in West Virginia until July, 1861. From there the 4th went to several brigades and corps before ending with Kimball's Independent Brigade in June 1865.

Truman had a number of brothers who fought in the Civil War, his brothers Gordon and John fought with the 18th U.S. Infantry. Gordon was killed at Stones River and John apparently died in the service. Unfortunately, John's military records are missing. Younger brothers Roswell and Emory served with the 145 Ohio National Guard for 100 days of service. This meant that five Beard brothers served in the Union.

Truman fought in most of the bloodiest and costliest battles of the Civil War. For four months in the winter of 1862-1863 Truman was sick at a hospital in Harpers Ferry, West Virginia thus missing the battle of Fredericksburg. Truman returned in time to fight in the battle of Chancellorsville, Virginia. At the battle of Chancellorsville, Confederate General Thomas "Stonewall" Jackson surprised General Oliver O. Howard's 11th Corps and rolled them up like a wet blanket and at the same battle Stonewall Jackson was shot by his own men and later died days later from pneumonia.

Then a few months later General Robert E Lee tried to invade the north. He was in Pennsylvania trying to draw the Union Army out in the open when the two armies met at Gettysburg. Truman was present at the battle that lasted three days ending with Lee's retreat back south. The 4th Ohio was mustered out of service July 12, 1865 regimental losses for the war were 8 officers and 95 enlisted men killed and mortally wounded; and 3 officers and 155 enlisted men died of disease; the total number of loss was 261.

Truman applied for and received a pension. He cites the time spent in the hospital and the difficult march to Gettysburg as the cause of his physical problems in later years. He continued to work as a blacksmith and among the correspondence in his pension file is a letter written by a person who must of disliked him – addressed the wife of the President, Mrs. Grover Cleveland, it request that Truman's pension be taken away, "…as he was healthy enough to work as a blacksmith and deliver mail." Truman died in 1903.

George W. Blackburn
1840 - 1929

George W. Blackburn served in Company A, of the 37th North Carolina Infantry Regiment, from November 20, 1861 to April 21, 1865. He fought in many battles including: New Bern on March 14, 1862; Hanover Court House; Fredericksburg; Chancellorsville; Petersburg; and Reams Station.

While trying to flank the Union advance at Petersburg, Company A was sent to secure the railroad station at Reams Station. A battle ensued, and Private George W. Blackburn was wounded on August 25, 1864. He returned to duty in September or October 1864. Due to his wounds, he was assigned to light duty, serving as a teamster, from November 1864 until February 1865. After the surrender of Confederate forces at Appomattox Court House, he remained in the custody of Union forces until his parole at Farmville, Virginia, April 21, 1865.

Upon his return to Ashe County, North Carolina, he found that the family farm had been burned and destroyed by the Union Army. George Married Caroline Green of Ashe County in 1866, and then moved to Fayette County, Ohio where he continued farming until his death in 1929.

Daniel Nathan Brobst
1834 - 1871

Daniel Nathan Brobst was born November 12th 1834 in Lynn Township, Lehigh County, Pennsylvania. He married Elizabeth Patterson in 1853. Daniel enlisted as a private in company B 39th Iowa Volunteers on August 26th 1862. The 39th Iowa was organized at Des Moines and Davenport and mustered in November 24th 1862.

The regiment's first action was the pursuit of Confederate General Nathan Bedford Forrest. They met up with Forrest at the battle of Parker's Cross Roads, and then the 39th guarded railroads until January of 1864. The regiment joined the Atlanta campaign and fought at the battles of Resaca and Allatoona under General William Tecumseh Sherman. They participated in the siege of Savannah whose defeat was presented as a Christmas gift to President Abraham Lincoln by General Sherman.

Daniel's regiment was also active in the campaign of the Carolinas and fought in the Salkehatchie Swamps. General Joseph Johnston was quoted as saying "I have not heard of such armies since the days of Julius Caesar," in remarking on how fast Sherman and his troops marched through the swamps. They fought at the battle of Bentonville, North Carolina and the 39th also occupied Raleigh until the surrender of Joseph Johnston's Army at the Bennett's house April 26th 1865.

The 39th Iowa marched into Washington D.C. for the Grand Review and mustered out on August 2, 1865. The total loss of the regiment was 6 officers and 58 enlisted men killed or mortally wounded; and 2 officers and 134 enlisted by disease; for a total loss to the regiment at 200.

Daniel Brobst died on April 22, 1871 at the age of 37.

Emmet Addis Brockway
1836 - 1912

Emmet Addis Brockway was born March 11, 1836 in Brockwayville, Pennsylvania.

Emmet joined the military on August 13, 1862 joining up with the 35th Iowa Volunteers, Company B. He mustered in at Camp Strong September 18,1862. He remained at Camp Strong until November 22, and then the Company moved to Cairo, Illinois, where they remained until December 19, 1862.

The unit participated in the siege of Vicksburg, where General Grant starved and battered the Confederates into submission. They surrendered on the 4th of July the same day that General Robert E Lee was retreating from Gettysburg. The 35th Iowa were also at: the battle of Pleasant Hill, Cane River Crossing, Yellow Bayou, Lake Chicot, Tupelo, and Nashville; the siege of Spanish Fort; and the assault and capture of Fort Blakely. The unit mustered out of service on August 10, 1865 the regiment lost 5 officers and 44 enlisted men killed and mortally wounded; 3 officers and 185 enlisted men by disease; the total men lost 237.

After the war Emmet married Jane Davisson on December 29, 1869. Emmet died on September 7, 1912 in Louisa County Iowa at the age of 76.

Theopholis Bonzo
1840 - 1896

Theopholis Bonzo was born on May 3, 1840; nicknamed "Tuft." He was the son of Peter Lewis Bonzo and Rebecca Brooks. According to the Beaver *Argus* of Oct 22, 1862, he was drafted in North Sewickley Township. He served in Company 6, 3rd Provost Regiment, Pennsylvania Cavalry, rose to the rank of sergeant and was busted back for disobedience, and then rose back up again.

He fought at the Battle of Gettysburg. He was captured November 19, 1863 at Stevensburg-Rapidan and ended up at Andersonville Prison in Georgia, where he was listed as "Sgt. T. L. Bunzo, Co. G, Regiment 18, Pennsylavania Cavalry." He paid his parole and was released November 20, 1864.

Returning to Beaver County, Pennsylvania, he married Sylvia Coleman Boots and they adopted Lucy Ethyl Penberthy. "Tuft" and Sylvia were principals involved in the founding and construction of the Wurtemburg United Methodist Church (still holding services today) near Ellwood City, Pennsylvania. "Tuft" rests in Presbyterian Cemetery, North Sewickley Township, Beaver County, Pennsylvania.

Thomas Bolton Burns
1846 - 1911

Thomas Bolton Burns, known as "Bolton," was born in Clarion County, Pennsylvania. Before the war he was a farmer. He enlisted with the 103rd Pennsylvania Volunteers, Company K at the age of 18. The regiment was formed at Camp Orr, Kittanning, Pennsylvania, known as the Armstrong County Fairgrounds, situated about a mile north of the town limits. The camp was enclosed by a high, tight board fence and no one was permitted to leave day or night without a pass issued by the regimental headquarters. Many eagerly volunteered and gathered early.

Much suffering occurred when the cold weather approached since the government was unable to furnish adequate clothing, camp and garrison equipment. To hasten recruiting, privates were given ten furlough days with a promise of another ten days provided they each brought in one or more men with them when they reported back for duty. A hundred men were furloughed at a time.

The 103rd Pennsylvania went into service as they advanced on Manassas, Virginia the regiment's battle list includes: Yorktown, Seven Days, Whitehall, and Goldsboro. At this point Thomas was on sick leave during the siege of Plymouth where the regiment was mostly captured and sent to Andersonville Prison. Thomas Burns escaped that fate and for medical reasons was transferred to the Veteran Reserve Corp. The 103rd Pennsylvania lost during it's service 3 officers and 50 enlisted men killed and mortally wounded; 1 officer and 352 enlisted men died of disease; for a total loss to the regiment of 406 men.

After the war Thomas married Mary Armstrong and lived in Adams County, Nebraska. Thomas "Bolton" Burns died in 1911.

John Adam Clark
1833 - 1907

John "Adam" Clark was born on September 9, 1833 at Jackson Center, Mercer County, Pennsylvania. In 1853 Adam worked for Ephraim Hunter in Plain Grove, Mercer County, and a year later on December 14, 1854 he married Elizabeth Jane Hunter the daughter of Ephraim. Once married Adam worked his father-in-law's farm for seven years and then beginning in 1861 and up to his enlistment in 1864 he worked for James Lawrence as a farmer and laborer.

Adam enlisted with the 212th/6th Pennsylvania Heavy Artillery, Company I on August 30 1864. He was 5' 10 ½" with brown eyes and dark complexion, some of the soldiers in the Company, Adam had known prior to his enlistment. The 6th Pennsylvania Heavy Artillery was organized at Pittsburgh, Pennsylvania on September 15, 1864 and they moved to Washington D.C. on September 17th 1864. There it was attached to the 2nd Brigade, DeRussy's Division, 22nd Corps until December of 1864 when it went to the 1st Brigade, DeRussy's Division, 22nd Corps to June, 1865. The 6th Pennsylvania guarded the Orange and Alexandria Railroad between Alexandria and Manassas, Virginia from September 29 to November 17, 1864. They garrisoned forts - Marcy, Ward, Craig, Aeno, Albany and Lyon and then the defenses of Washington D.C. south of the Potomac until June, 1865. At the time they mustered out on June 13, 1865 the unit lost during service 2 enlisted men killed; and 44 by disease, for a total of 46.

After Adam was discharged in June of 1865 he returned to Mercer County to work for James Lawrence. Then he moved to Coal Burg, and worked for the coal bank. In April 1882 he moved to Hartford, Trumbull County, Ohio and died there in 1907. He is buried in Center Cemetery, Brookfield, Trumbull County, Ohio.

Hiram Consla
1817-1889

Prior to 1820 Hiram moved from New York to Crawford County, Pennsylvania with his parents, Andrew and Debbie Consla and his brother, Peter. Hiram served in Union Army during the Civil War. He enlisted with 150th Pennsylvania Volunteers, Company C.

Enlisting in Philadelphia, June 20th 1864, his name was misspelled as Hiram Consolo, and appears as such on his pension papers. During the battle of North Anna Hiram suffered a neck wound. During the battle of Petersburg July 6, 1864 Hiram Consla deserted for reasons unknown.

He married Lydia White in 1848 and supported his family by farming. They had two sons, Henry and Samuel. He died in 1889, in Watson Run, Crawford County, Pennsylvania.

Josiah Coulter
1839 - 1913

Josiah Coulter, son of the Robert and Hannah Coulter was born November 25, 1839 in Salem Township, Mercer County, Pennsylvania. His Great-Grandfather, Archibald Coulter, was a land owner of note just after the American Revolutionary War in the Gettysburg, Pennsylvania area.

Josiah Coulter enlisted on October 6, 1861 at Meadville, Pennsylvania and mustered in on November 25, 1861 at Philadelphia, Pennsylvania. At the time of his enlistment he was as a Private in Company I, 59th Regiment, Second Pennsylvania Cavalry and was to serve three years. He was promoted to Corporal on November 1, 1862 and honorably discharged December 16, 1863. He re-enlisted as a Veteran Volunteer in the same Company and Regiment. Promoted to Sergeant on December 8, 1864, he was mustered out and honorably discharged on July 13, 1865 at Clouds Mill, Virginia, from Company I, First Pennsylvania Provisional Cavalry to which he was transferred by consolidation as a Sergeant.

Josiah Coulter's first battle was at Cedar Mountain on August 9, 1862, followed by the Second Battle of Bull Run where he had a horse shot out from under him. He was in two days of fighting on August 29 and 30. On the night of the 30th, the 59th Regiment held the famous Stone Bridge at Centreville, Virginia. He then did scout work and was in several skirmishes. His regiment took part in the Battle

of Chancellorsville, Virginia on May 2 and 3, 1863. On July 1, 1863 he arrived at Gettysburg, Pennsylvania and was assigned as a guard at General Meade's Headquarters. He claimed to have fought on his Great-Grandfather's farm, located between the Union lines at Gettysburg and the cavalry battlefield. Only July 3rd at 24:00 his regiment was sent with 2,500 prisoners to Westminster, Virginia, returning on July 5. On July 7th they went across the Potomac River into Virginia. On December 16, 1863 he was honorably discharge. He re-enlisted in the same company and regiment receiving a veteran's furlough then returned to his home to marry Beulah Williams, eldest daughter of John and Margaret Williams, on February 21, 1864. She was born in Greenwood Township, Crawford County, Pennsylvania on December 19, 1841. He returned to his regiment and fought in the Battle of the Wilderness on May 5th through 12th during which time his regiment flanked the enemy between the Wilderness and Richmond, Virginia tearing up rail lines and retreating towards the James River.

He participated in the battle of Spotsylvania, Virginia on May 12 to 21, fighting more or less for fourteen days before reaching gunboats on the James River. After the battle of Cold Harbor on July 12, his next battle was Petersburg, Virginia. After fighting for one day and in the thick of the battle at Petersburg, on July 12, 1864 his squad was fighting near a swampy stream trying to cross a bridge ahead of the rebels. In the dash all except Josiah Coulter made it. His horse was killed and he received a leg injury. He tried to "fake" an appearance of being dead but the rebels examined him to see where he was hit, found him alive and took him prisoner on July 12, 1864, at Lees Mill. He had

Josiah Coulter
1839 - 1913

received five slight wounds and had participated in eight battles and eleven skirmishes. The prison records show he was first taken to Libby Prison at Richmond, Virginia and was there one day, July 14, 1964. From there he was sent to Andersonville Prison arriving July 16, 1864. On November 13, 1864 he was then transferred to Millen Prison and to Savannah, Georgia where he was exchanged November 26, 1864 at the mouth of the Savannah River. There he took a ship for Camp Parole near Annapolis, Maryland which took seven days.

It was one of these injuries in the back of the leg which served to benefit him in gaining his release from prison and subsequent exchange. While at Andersonville he and others attempted to tunnel out of the prison, using a broken case knife to cut away roots as, "large as a man's leg," and a pant leg to carry away the sand. They had tunneled under the stockade and had started toward the surface when the prisoner exchange was made. An old prisoner gave him a staff because he was highly esteemed by his comrades and was counted a good soldier and a hard fighter. Arriving home December 19, 1864 he weighed only 92 pounds. When taken prisoner he weighed 175 pounds. After recuperating he again started for his regiment getting as far as Washington when General Lee surrendered his army on April 9, 1865. On April 13, 1865 he was sent to Camp Distribution, Virginia. He received an honorable discharge at Clouds Mill, Virginia on July 17, 1865.

He established his home in Greenwood Township, Crawford County, Pennsylvania, raising a family of five girls and four boys. He was a charter member of the Elijah Thompson G.A.R. Post No. 417 of Shekleyville, Pennsylvania, organized in the fall of 1883 and receiving their Charter April 2, 1884.

Second Pennsylvania Calvary - 25th Reunion

Josiah Coulter
1839 - 1913

Josiah Coulter later wrote about his experiences during the Civil War in the following letter:

I enlisted Oct. 1861 in Co. 3 or 52nd, Pa. Cavalry as a private soldier. Was discharged July 14, 1865 a first seargent. I was in eight solad battles the first battle that I went thru was the second batle of Bull Run, Va. then Spotselvania Court house, Kole haror, Shantille, Cedar mountains, Getesburgm, battle of the Wilderness fought 2 days and one night was relieved the second nite got our horses and road all nite flanked rebel army between the wildenis and Richmond tore up the ralrod then retreated for the James River fought more or less for fourteen day before we got too our gun boats on the James river. I had one horse shot and killed at the battle of bull run an the 12 day of July 1864 fought one day at the Battle of Petersburgh had my horse shot and was taken Prisner that day. I was taken to Leibey prisen at Richmond Va. was thar 6 days then taken to Andersonville July 23 left Andersonville on the 3 day of November 1866 and was then taken to Mellon prison then taken to Savanah Ga. on the 25 day of November was exchanged at the mouth of the Savanah River. Took the vecel for Anapolis, Marlon. Was 5 days on the boat. On the 19th day of December I got home when I was taken prisner I wayed 175 when I got home I wayed 92 lbs. I got 5 slight wounds, was in 8 battles went thru the whole fite fought one day at Petersburg was in 11 skirmishes and fought 14 da. Our rigement fot a whole then fell back and another regiment took thar place. That was the way we maid our escaoe to the James River.

He died May 13, 1913 and is interred, along with his wife who died September 18, 1919, at Porters Corners Cemetery east of Atlantic, Pennsylvania.

17

ALEXANDER TARLTON CRAIG
1839 - 1906

Alexander Tarlton Craig was a young farmer in Northern Armstrong County near the town of Tidal, with his new wife and his widowed Mother when he was drafted into the army in September of 1862. His three older brothers - Samuel, William, and James enlisted in September of 1861. He was detached as a private with Company B, 46th Pennsylvania Volunteers from September 1863 to July 1864. According to his own account he did most of his fighting under General Joseph Hooker. After the Battle of Gettysburg, on July 18, 1863 the 46th Regiment went by rail to Nashville. Here the First Division was detailed to guard the Nashville and Chattanooga Railroad from Tullahoma to Bridgeport. The country through which the railroad passes was infested with guerrillas and rebel cavalry, ever watchful for an opportunity to destroy the railroad and to wreck the track. It was vital to the existence of the army that this line should be kept open, and that it should be operated to its fullest capacity. The vigilance and fidelity with which this service was preformed on the part of the 46th won the approval of its superior officers. Sometime during this operation, probably between September and November 1863, Alexander came down with scurvy and diarrhea and lay ill along the tracks for 4 to 6 weeks according to one of his letters.

General W.F. Smith and Joe Hooker executed a coup October 26-29 that restored a sorely need supply line on the Tennessee River so General Grant could move by late November 1863. The next big battle would be at Lookout Mountain near Chattanooga - the fight was known as the "battle above the clouds". On November 24, 1863 when Hooker drove the Confederates from Lookout Mountain, however a day later General Sherman could still not make any headway against Missionary Ridge from its northern end, So Grant ordered the center to advance. General Thomas' men with Philip Sheridan conspicuous among them displayed great courage proceeding to carry Bragg's position at the top; there Hookers forces joined them in routing the confederates. By nightfall General Bragg was in full retreat to Georgia. The victory left Chattanooga in Union hands for the rest of the war. Early in January 1864 a large portion of the officers and men of the 46th Regiment having re-enlisted for a second term of three years keeping it intact as an organization they were given a veteran furlough and returned to Pennsylvania. It was unlikely that Alexander Craig received a furlough, since he had only served for six months. Upon the veteran's return the division rejoined the corps in winter quarters in and around Chattanooga.

In a letter Alexander wrote, they marched to Atlanta on the sixth of May 1864 as part of Sherman's army with seventy thousand strong and one-hundred and fifty cannon packed up their winter quarters and began the memorable Atlanta Campaign. At Dolton, where Joseph E. Johnston, who commanded the Rebel Army, was first met and was turned out of a position by nature and a well fortified position through Snake Creek Gap, which had already been captured by Geary's division. Following up the retreating enemy Sherman found him well positioned at Resaca, prepared to dispute his further progress here Sherman again attempted a movement by the right flank, but Johnston taking advantage of his enemies wreaked lines in front, delivered a heavy and well sustained attack; falling upon the division of Hooker and Schofield. He found Hooker not prepared for the encounter and after a bloody conflict, Johnston was driven with a loss of four guns and many prisoners.

Alexander Tarlton Craig
1839 - 1906

In this engagement the 46th Pennsylvania sustained three men killed and five wounded. Pushing the enemy steadily back, on the 25th of May the regiment was again engaged at Pumpkinvine Creek and at New Hope Church. The country was broken and the enemy well entrenched his lines stretching across Lost Pine and Kennesaw Mountains from Dallas to Marietta, presenting an unbroken front. From the 25th of May near the middle of June, Sherman always fruitful in resources operated against the enemy lines compelling him by constant battering and picket firing, and by frequent assaults gradually to give ground, taking first Pine Knob, then Lost Mountain, the length the long line of breast works connecting the latter with Kennesaw Mountain. Finally on the 22nd of June the enemy finding himself slowly but surely pushed from his strong position assumed the offensive and made a furious attack on Joe Hookers Corps in position near Club House. It fell upon Knipes Brigade and was led by General John Bell Hood but failed. Hood was repulsed with heavy losses including some prisoners. "Williams Division," says General Thomas in his official report, "skirmished itself into position on the right of Geary's Division, the right of Williams resting at Culp's House on the Powder Spring and Marietta Road. About 4 P.M. the enemy in heavy force, attacked Knipe's Brigade in its advanced position, before his men had time to throw up any works and withdrew their ranks hopelessly broken, each assault having been repelled with heavy loss." In the various engagements at Dallas, Pine Knob, Kennesaw Mountain and Marietta, in all of which the 46th participated in, the loss was fourteen killed and about 30 wounded.

This is about the time in late June 1864 that Alexander T. Craig has another attack with diarrhea and scurvy, as were a great number of men. On 16th of July, Sherman crossed the Chattahoochee River and sweeping around to the left, began closing in upon Atlanta. Alexander was sent back to the hospital at Chattanooga and was treated for 10 to 12 days then he was sent onto Browns General Hospital in Louisville, Kentucky. There he was treated for three month. He then received a 30 day furlough from this hospital from September 26 to October 26th. After his return he was sent to a hospital at Pittsburgh, Pennsylvania, where he stayed for three months, from November 1864 until January 24, 1865. He was then sent to the Invalid Corps in Cincinnati, Ohio Company K, 6th Regiment V.R.C. from Jan.24th to June 30 1865.

ALEXANDER TARLTON CRAIG
1839 - 1906

It was at this time that he wrote a letter to his General, Joseph Hooker, about having not receiving any pay for 16 months:

> *Dear sir:*
>
> *I am a private of Co. K 6 V.R.C. formally of Co B 46th P.A. Vols. Intended then a drafted man in 1863 and has been with them up till last fall when I was obliged to leave on account of ill health but that could not help. I was sent to Pittsburgh PA. Then I was put in the invalid corps. Were I have been all winter. Now that the war is over I would like to go home so I know of no one that I can ask to do me a favor better than you. I want to state my case and I hope you won't take it hard of me asking you if it was not a case of need I would not do so. There was 4 brothers of us three of them went volunteer and I was left at home to support my wife child, mother and two sisters by my own hands on my farm. Since I have been gone the farm has been idle. I have had no pay for 16 months they having not much when I left. I ask you as the war is over and if you don't think I ought to be home as there are much need for either me or my money. I ask you to consider and do for me your pleasure. I have done the most of my fighting under you so I hope you won't go back on me now in time of need it is all in your power whether I get home or not. No person home with my family nor hasn't been since I left and me the only son left to support my mother and children. I have stated my case clearly to you so you can act as you think proper but I hope you will act in my favor. I acknowledge your humble servant Alexander T. Craig Please excuse me a private, soldier for writing to you.*
>
> *Yours?*
> *Alexander T. Craig*
> *Co. K 6 V.D.C. Cincinnati Ohio*

According to letters he wrote on October 4, 1880, to his wife Mary Elizabeth Metzger, whom he had married on September 22, 1860; and Meredith J. P., September 22, 1906, when he came home from war with a beard nobody recognizing him. He was not able to do anything for more than two years because of general disability. He got some help by taking Keastaters or Kostetters [?] bitters. At this time he received a pension of $12.00 a month.

On December 15, 1890 he made a Declaration for Increase of an Invalid Pension stating that he was still suffering from scurvy and disease of the mouth and chronic diarrhea, disease of liver and piles and could not work. Although, when he got feeling a little stronger he drove his team in the summer, but balance of the time he had to get a driver for his team. Alexander was treated by Doctor McDowell of Rimersburg, Pennsylvania for these illnesses. Dr. Norman of Pittsburgh also recommended he continue to take the Kostetters bitters, since it gave him some relief. This Declaration was signed by Josiah Callens and T.T. Meredith, and G.W. Hines. He would continue to receive a disability check from the Government until his death on June 28, 1906. After his death his wife applied for his disability and she received $50.00 a month until her death in 1927. In her application she stated her farm of 66 acres was being rented out for about $50.00. A sum she declared that was hardly enough for her to live on although, she did have some interests coming in from the money she had in the bank.

Wilson Dean
1838 - 1911

Wilson Dean was born on October 29, 1838 in Mercer (later Lawrence) County, Pennsylvania. He married Mary Muse on July 1, 1858. Wilson was a farmer for most of his life in New Lebanon, Pennsylvania. He joined Company A of the 139th Pennsylvania Volunteers as a musician. The 139th Pennsylvania was organized at Pittsburgh on September 1st, 1862. The regiment traveled to Washington D.C. September 1-3. Their first assignment was to bury the dead at Bull Run (Manassas) battlefield in Virginia.

At the battle of Antietam they were held in reserve. The 139th Pennsylvania remained with the Army of the Potomac and served throughout all the fighting from 1862 to 1865 sustaining a total loss of 10 officers and 135 enlisted men killed and mortally wounded; and 5 officers and 86 enlisted men who died of disease, for a total of 236 deaths.

Wilson after the war went back to farming, but an affliction of rheumatism contracted from exposure during the war greatly affected his health and his ability to work. The 139th was conveyed from Brandy Station, Virginia to Washington D.C. in open train cars traveling in bad weather in December of 1863. The fact regarding this are well documented in his pension file. Wilson voted the Republican ticket and was a member of A.O.U.W, No. 54 of New Lebanon and the Norval Muse Post No. 251 of the Grand Army of the Republic. The G.A.R. Post was dedicated to his wife's brother who was killed in the Chancellorsville campaign in the battle near Salem Church, Fredericksburg, Virginia on May 3, 1863. Norval was also a member of the 139th Pennsylvania. Wilson died on March 1, 1911 and is buried in New Lebanon.

JOHN BURRIS FAY
1833 - 1879

Captain John Burris Fay was was born in Center County, Pennsylvania on June 17, 1833. He was married to Mary Jane "Mollie" Baker. The life and service of John Burris Fay is detailed in this biographical sketch that appeared after his death by the Independent Order of Odd Fellows:

In pursuance of call, the Odd Fellows met at their hall on Wednesday evening to make arrangements to receive the remains of Capt. John B. Fay, of Louisville, Ky. On Thursday a large number of the brethren met at the hall and proceeded in a body to the depot to meet the remains, which arrived on train 12. They were taken to the 1st M. E. Church, where a short discourse was delivered by the Rev. T L Flood and the remains were viewed by a number of his numerous friends. At the grave, the beautiful ceremonies of the Order were observed. C. R. Marsh, Esq. acting at N.G., and L. W. Hannen, Esq., as chaplain. The pall bearers were Messrs. J. F. Frazier, T. J. Doyle, E. Woodring, Geo. V. Dreutlein, Robert Andrews and John B. Compton. The remains were in charge of King and Long, undertakers, of this city. The deceased was born in Centre County, Pennsylvania June 17, 1833. He was left fatherless when about one year old, and his mother subsequently married Philip Harpst, a well-known citizen of this place. In the year 1839, Capt. Fay first became a citizen of this place with his parents, that being the date of their first settlement here. During the year 1845 or 6 the deceased began to learn the printing trade in the office of the "Gazette," published by L. L. Lord in this city, which paper afterwards merged into the "Crawford Journal." In this office he worked until George Youngson started the "Cussewago Chronicle," when he went into the office of that paper, and continued to work their until it suspended publication. In 1851 or 52 he, in company with Harper Mitchell, started the "Spirit of the Age," which paper was the predecessor of the Meadville Republican. After this time he was engaged in the office of the "Crawford Democrat" and the "Crawford Journal" until the year 1858, when he learned the photograph business, then in its infancy, and became one of the most skillful and successful artists in the city. In August, 1862, he recruited company C, 150th Regiment, Pennsylvania Volunteers, of which he was elected captain. Soon after entering service he was appointed Brigade Inspector, in which capacity he served until after the battle of Chancellorsville when, his health failing him, he was transferred to the Invalid Corps, where he served in the capacity of captain until the close of the war. Soon

Molly Baker

John Burris Fay
1833 - 1879

after his discharge he moved to Dayton, Ohio, where he engaged in a business of Steam Laundry and gentlemen's furnishing goods. Owing to adverse circumstances he failed in the business there, but magnanimously refused to claim the benefit of any exemption or bankrupt laws. Surrendering up everything he had in the way of worldly effects, he again entered the printing office as a journeyman, and continued to work at his old trade until he had secured enough to start in the photography business, when he opened a gallery in Louisville, where he remained until he died. He has been in poor health for a number of years. He leaves a wife and one son about 19 years of age. His mother resides in this section, and he has also three half-brothers and four half-sisters, in this neighborhood. He was a member of Boone Lodge No. 1, I.O. of O.F. of Louisville, Ky., also a member of the Masonic fraternity. The remains were enclosed in a very handsome casket, and the top was placed with some beautiful floral offerings. One in the design of and anchor was presented by the Lodge of Odd Fellows to which he belonged. Another in the design of a compass and square, with a card attached bearing the inscription, "Sympathy of Fall City Lodge, No 386."

A. Y. M.

Richard R. Gardner
- 1886

Richard R. Gardner was a Civil War Veteran, serving with Company I, 100th Regiment, Pennsylvania Volunteers, "The Roundheads." He joined on August 31, 1861. In the Samuel P. Bates' 1870 history, *Pennsylvania Volunteers*, Richard Gardner is listed as unaccounted for in the roster.

Richard Gardner was married to Elizabeth Elliott. They were the parents of six children. He died March 9, 1886 and is buried in Greenwood Cemetery in New Castle.

Reuben George
1837 - 1906

Reuben George was the son of Martin L. and Anna Davis George of Mercer County. His wife, Mary Jane was the daughter of Benjamin and Sarah Longwell Miller of Clarion County. Reuben and Mary Jane George lived in East Brady, Clarion County. Reuben was born November 20, 1837 in Mercer County. Mary Jane Miller was born April 9, 1844.

Reuben joined the 78th Pennsylvania Volunteers, Company E on August 28, 1862 for 3 years. His occupation at the time was that of a laborer. Reuben was mustered out September 11, 1865. Reuben's pension file reveals that he received disability benefits in the amount of $12.00 per month until his death because of piles and chronic diarrhea after returning from the war. Several sworn affidavits in the file from various friends, his physician and brother, Victor, state he was in perfect health before the war and after his return he was unable to do manual labor due to his condition. He did not apply for a disability pension until 1887. At the time owned the hotel - The Monterey House.

In 1897 Reuben attended the reunion at Chickamauga. Three years later his son Christian Ellsworth George was killed by a train. Reuben George died on July 29, 1906.

Joseph Groff
1821 - 1903

Joseph Groff was born on October 21, 1821 in New London, Lancaster County. He worked for the B. & O. Railroad from approximately 1839 to 1850. He married Rebecca Beichtel on October 28, 1842 in Hollidaysburg, Blair County, Pennsylvania. She died on August 13, 1850 in Harper's Ferry, possibly from cholera. After his wife's death Joseph left Harper's Ferry, taking their daughter, Rebecca, who was sickly from smallpox, to live with the William and Margaret (Smith) Carmack family in Woodsboro, Maryland. He resided in Frederick County, Maryland with his son, William, through 1851. On January 1, 1852 he married Susan Christina Smith (sister of Margaret Carmack) in Frederick. Joseph and Susan live in Walkersville, Frederick County, Maryland around 1853. They had ten children, eight of whom survived to adulthood. Between 1858 and 1861 they lived in Philadelphia, Pennsylvania where he owned a stockyard and a hotel. Early in 1861 they moved back to Frederick, Maryland and opened a store selling goods at public auction.

At the outbreak of the Civil War the town of Frederick (like Maryland) was a divided town (half supported the Union and half the South). Joseph had a gigantic American flag he hung outside his store that extended to another building he owned across the street as a way to demonstrate his support of the Union. The secessionists opposed this display of the flag. A large crowd confronted Joseph, demanding he take it down. He refused and the crowd declared they would return with the town's strongest man, Mr. Poffinberger, to force Joseph to remove the flag. Joseph stated, "... if any

Joseph Groff
1821 - 1903

man took that flag he would have me to whip first, and if that man came into do it, I would meet him." Mr. Poffinberger or the crowd never returned and the flag remained.

The Brengle Home Guard Company of Frederick City was formed April 24, 1861 - headed by Major Richard Potts and Captain J. Alfred F. Brengle. The Company was composed of Union defenders from Frederick and they were commissioned on June 7, 1861 by Governor Thomas H. Hicks. Joseph Groff joined and was made a Third Lieutenant. Their duties included guarding the Monocracy Railroad Bridge.

On August 21, 1861, at the Old Market House, Joseph enlisted as a First Lieutenant, Company B of 1st Potomac Home Brigade of the Maryland Infantry Regiment of Volunteers. At the same time his oldest son, William, enlisted in the same regiment and company. William served as a private and later was promoted to corporal in the unit. Joseph also recruited some sixty-two men for Company "B". He took with him, his prized large U.S. flag. The Regiment's officers were: Colonels William P. Maulsby, Roger E. Cook, Lt. Cols. George R. Dennis, John A. Steiner, Charles J. Brown and Majors John I. Yellott and Eugene C. Baugher. The regiment was organized in Frederick on August 15, 1861, and then mustered into the United States service by Major Smith - U.S. Army on Friday, September 6, 1861 at 4 o'clock PM. and by December 13, 1861 for three years service.

During the period December 1861 until April 1862 the regiment was lead by General Banks. They trained and were first quartered on Barracks Hill near Frederick. In the winter of 1861 they left the barracks and wintered at Camp Worman, north of Frederick. By the spring of 1862 the forces marched up the Shenandoah Valley as far as Winchester. Then they were assigned to guarding the Baltimore and Ohio railroad line. General Banks and his troops were driven out of the Shenandoah Valley and assigned to the Harper's Ferry area. After the second battle of Bull Run, the regiment guarded the passages along the Potomac River near the mouth of the Monocacy and then concentrated their efforts at Harper's Ferry. On September 15, 1862, after being surrounded by Confederate forces at Harper's Ferry the regiment surrendered. The soldiers, including Lt. Joseph Groff, were marched to Camp Parole near Annapolis. Along the way Joseph managed to bury his large U.S. flag (which he carried with him) under a rock on the Potomac River shore so it wouldn't fall into Rebel hands. The Union soldiers were paroled and exchanged the next day.

The regiment was then assigned to duty at Alexandria, Virginia, and along the Potomac in the southern part of Maryland. Joseph did go back as soon as possible to retrieve the flag but it was gone. On February 10, 1863, Lt. Joseph Groff was made a Captain of Company "B" when Captain Glessner resigned. During May 1863, Captain Groff was in command over the Potomac from Port Tobacco to Point Lookout, at Chapel Point in Charles County, Maryland. One night while two of his soldiers, Private Sylvester Stockman and his brother, Private Lattimer Stockman and Private Charles Keeler approached three men "under a fodder shock" in a feed shed (Jones' Barn). The Confederates, Simpson and Brown, surrendered right away but the third, Watt Bowie, managed to escape. The

Joseph Groff
1821 - 1903

Union patrol took their two prisoners back towards company headquarters when another fellow came up to the group and joined them thinking they were some friends of his. By the time he realized his mistake he was also captured by Captain Groff's soldiers. That last prisoner taken was a Confederate Major, Charles C. Hume, but his rank was unknown to the Union patrol because of the large overcoat Hume wore. Continuing on the march back to headquarters Major Hume started up a conversion with his guards and asked about the Union command the two soldiers belonged to, at which point his mind raced to previous events months earlier. He exclaimed to Captain Groff's troops that they had been taken prisoners at Harper's Ferry by Confederate troops and had not been exchanged. Major Hume yelled, "I will kill you both!" and suddenly pulled out a hidden pistol and fired at Sylvester Stockman, wounding his hand. In spite of a bloodily hand, Sylvester was able to fire back and Hume fell dead from the shot. The gun's ball entered the Major's left side; hit a brass button causing the musket ball and button to travel through the Major's body to his backbone. Only after checking on Hume's condition did they realize he was a Confederate officer. The other two Confederate prisoners threw up their hands and yelled, "For God's sake, don't shoot us!" Sylvester and Lattimer Stockman were able to keep the other prisoners under control and get them back to their Union headquarters. Captain Groff praised his young men for keeping calm and doing their duty. The captured prisoners turned out to be blockade runners. Their illegal supplies were later located and turned over to General Lockwood at Point Lookout. Major Hume's body was brought to headquarters, the button-ball laboriously removed from his body by Captain Groff. A large gold ring and a hefty sum of money were additionally removed from the Major's body. He was buried in a nearby churchyard, Pickawaxon Church, in Charles County, Maryland. After the War, a brother of Major Charles Hume met with Captain Groff in Washington, D.C. to hear an account of his brother's death.

A Groff family story is that Capt. Groff stopped in Woodsboro, Maryland on his way to Gettysburg in June 1863 to kiss his daughter (Rebecca) good-bye. At the time the First Regiment Potomac Home Brigade of Maryland was lead by Colonel William P. Maulsby. They marched from Baltimore, via Frederick City to reach Gettysburg. They arrived at 8 a.m. on July 2nd. Near midnight of July 2nd, a skirmish between both sides broke out as soldiers from both sides tried to get water for their canteens at Spangler's Spring, which was near Culp's Hill. During the early morning hours of Friday, July 3, 1863, Colonel Maulsby's regiment was selected to engage the enemy within the woods. The forest areas were entered and the enemy engaged and driven back behind a stone wall, which was nearly parallel with the turnpike. During the battle around mid-day while leading his men at Spangler's Spring, a bullet to the right foot wounded Capt. Joseph Groff. But there was no time to remove the bullet, only time enough to put a dressing over the wound. From the field hospital, Captain Groff returned to the battlefield and reported to Colonel Maulsby. The Regiment had 80 men killed or wounded and their ammunition was in short supply. The Brigade Commander of the 2nd Brigade, 1st Division, Henry H. Lockwood, wrote in his report, "I cannot too strongly comment the courage and good conduct of every officer and man engaged in this fearful enterprise." Captain Joseph Groff was given permission late on July 3, 1863 to return to his home in Frederick, since it was so close to Gettysburg, to have a surgeon remove the bullet. It took four months for his wound to heal. Joseph returned to his company and active duty by November 2, 1863. His son William was unharmed in the battle.

JOSEPH GROFF
1821 - 1903

Joseph was in charge of his Company "B" at Sandy Hook then made Provost Marshall near Point of Rocks. One of his duties including returning to Frederick and ordering the entire town's people to remain in their homes. By July and August of 1864, Captain Groff became quite ill and was allow time to recuperate at his home in Frederick. Back in the battlefield by late August 1864 he also suffered from hearing lost due to explosives. His son William suffered from typhoid fever. Both father and son were honorably discharged in Washington, D.C. on December 20, 1864. Captain Groff returned to his home in Frederick.

After the war he became quite the entrepreneur - he operated the Groff Hotel in Frederick; owned Brodbeck Hall, with its 28 acres (the property included a clubhouse and a beer garden and a farm to produce vegetables for his clients at the Groff Hotel. The land was later renamed Groff Park, flowers were also produced in a greenhouse on the property.) In 1870, he sold a house and land in Johnsville, Maryland (located between Libertytown and Union Bridge) and his real estate holdings were valued at $22,000 and had a personal savings of $4,000. He also built a brickyard in Frederick at the southeast corner of Eighth and Market Streets and the clay was dug from a quarry near his livery stable. His new Groff House was started in 1884 using bricks made by the brickyard. It covered 707 to 709 North Market Street and also served as his family's home and one of Frederick's grand hotels.

He remained active in local politics, supporting the Republican Party, but behind the scenes. He applied in November 24, 1879 and received a veteran's pension (#180772 - 281584) of $15 a month. On October 2, 1899 he was selected as the President of the Rossbourg Club of Maryland Agricultural College. He lived, until his death on February 12, 1903, in his landmark Groff House in Frederick. He died of apoplexy which he had 2 days along with general paralysis. He was 82 years old. Captain Groff was buried at Mt. Olivet Cemetery, Frederick, MD. Family members continued to live at the Groff House, including his daughter, Nannie Groff, until her death in May 1948.

John Hardenbrook
1847 - 1938

John Huse Hardenbrook was born on July 20, 1847 in Madison, Indiana. Before the war he was listed as a miner. He enlisted to fight in the Civil War as a private in Company H, 137th Indiana Volunteers after he learned of his brother, Lewis' death at Missionary Ridge, Tennessee on 25th of November. Lewis was decapitated by a cannon ball and was buried where he fell he died at the age of 23. John was married at 8 p.m. and left for war at 11p.m.

Organized at Indianapolis, Indiana the 137th was ordered to Tennessee and assigned to guard the railroad in the Tennessee and Alabama Department of the Cumberland until September of 1864 when they were mustered out of service on September 21, 1864.

John re-enlisted with the 20th U.S. Infantry, Company D, he went first to Richmond, Virginia and then to New Orleans via an Atlanta transport. John encountered violent storms off Cape Hatteras and was officially listed as lost at sea. A boat called the *Evening Star* was sunk a few weeks before. Finally his boat docked at New Orleans. He was later transferred to Fort Ransom, South Dakota were he fought in the Sioux uprising. He was captured by Indians but escaped with an Indian scout. John was shot at many times but was never wounded.

After the war John married Philinda Katherine Montgomery on March 15, 1870 and traveled by covered wagon to Dallas County, Iowa where they settled in Beaver Township and later moved to Minburn, named Sugar Grove. They would live there until 1907 when they moved to Linden, Iowa. In Linden everyone called John "Dad." He was a member of the Greenville Lodge Camp 75,

John Hardenbrook
1847 - 1938

Des Moines, Iowa an organization for Civil War veterans. John died in 1938. The following poem was written by his granddaughter at the time of his death:

Grandfathers chair is vacant now.
His memory we will always keep.
For taps have sounded our heads we bow.
As we lay him down to sleep.
The twisted cord on his battered hat,
Meant more to him by far,
He wouldn't trade it for all the world.
It's his relic of the G.A.R.
The blue vest sagged with the medals he wore.
Each one had a story to tell.
His musket hung above the door.
It had served him very well.
We loved the yarns he told.
Seems I hear his voice again.
You folks may think I'm getting old,
But I can fight with the best of them.
We are sorry to lose these grand old men,
Whose fame is written in the stars?
We know they will meet again,
At the reunion of the G.A.R.

John at age 90

WILLIAM HARDENBROOK
1836 - 1919

He was born on July 12, 1836 in Woodford, Kentucky as James William Hardenbrook, but was always called William. He married Sarah J. Raiser on March 17, 1857. He died on September 26, 1919, at the age of 82. He wrote this autobiographical letter to the *Madison Courier*:

Dear Courier,

Having long ago taken Horace Greeley's advice, I am away out here in God's country and feel like talking to or about those I knew in your pretty city on Auld Lang Syne. Being alone now in the world nothing to do but read or write, as my rambling mind carries me back to 1847 when I first landed at the old Madison wharf on the old steamboat Blue Wing. The next year father enlisted and went with Capt. John T. Hughes to Mexico. Also John Tagues father in the same Co. and regiment 4 under General Taylor. Leaving their families to root hog or die. I being the oldest went to work as a cotton bug in the old Counden factory under Eastman their foreman. Not liking that I went to Daddy Reed in the Old Madison House at 4 dollars a month, blacking boots and using a wheel barrow for a dray going from hotel to boats and depot. Cleared about 15 dollars to 20 dollars a month keeping mother and the younger children in clothes and plenty to eat. Then the big Madison Hotel being built, I got a job there in the dining room at 12 dollars a month then tips added. J. Dunn not Dutch Henry Staul head porter, Jake Smith and wife head cooks. I was then promoted to boot jack and assistant porter. Cripple Frank Sheets and Bill Woods, clerks Bob Browning and John Doble proprietors. I got to be head porter and clerk master and transfer agent in bus line and transferring of all baggage. So mother and children did not need for anything and Billy had plenty and end to friends. So ever since about 62 years I wonder who I would recognize there? For instance Bill Kirchner, Bill Phibbs, Robert Right Reas and all the Reas with Jim Buchanan, Bill Keuthan, I stripped tobacco for him. and Jake and Andy Fisher, worked for the Dallies and Copeland Wies on the buses. When my rambling mood came on I went to the steamer Wisconsin as second steward Afterwards I went on to the Golden Gate which I was head steward of for 2 and a half years. Capt. Stapp and Bill Stapp clerk. Followed the Ohio awhile then Louisville to St. Louis, then to New Orleans and St. Louis also up Red River on the steamers Golden Gate, Pat Whitson Navigator Jesse K. Bell, Eclipse on A.L. Shotwell salary from 60 dollars to 125 a month, yet remembering mother and children at home. My home was where ever my hat was. Finally I became tired of rambling. I married in 1857, quit the river in 1859 and moved to Morgan Co. Ind. going there for my better health. War broke out, and being a Freemont Republican I could not stand

WILLIAM HARDENBROOK
1836 - 1919

it. Father and brothers and my wife's father and all her brothers gone. I kissed my sweet wife and 2 sweet babes and went as a private July 22, 1862. Aug. 12, 1862 was ministered in as first Lieutenant, Co H 70th Ind. Vol Inf, with noble Ben Harrison with who my wife was intimate. I served until the close of war and came home as Captain and Provost Marshall Third Division 20th Army Corps. Wounded 6 times, 3 severe wounds I suffer with yet, but now at my age I don't mind it, I have not a enemy in the world of which I know. I visit about with my children go where and when I please. I do not owe a dollar. have plenty to eat and wear. My beloved companion after 4 or 5 years of illness was laid to rest April 12, after a happy union of 52 years. She only awaits my coming God bless her which will be when I answer the call. The family is now scattered all over the world. mother and sister are in your cemetery there, father, Irvin, wife's mother and four sons at Louisville, also Newton, Kansas. Wellington, Kansas and Hinton cemeteries where I will finally rest. So in conclusion I can view your little town and Old Michigan Road, Schmidts store building and the Old High school on a high knob where I went when I could and the Catholic Church near the foot of the hill. The fair grounds and old John Broughs engine with cogs in the center of the track to pull up the hill. And what fun I used to have helping the Jenkins pull the seins to catch fish and they would give me all I could carry and let me have their skiffs to go across the river to Ky. and get wild blackberries for which we got 50 cents a bucket. Could I live my days over Rockefeller and Vanderbilt would not be in it. So my advice to a young man is just to stick. That is a big word. and a logical motto. Just study it some of you old fellows of my age and write me. I have a dear sister and nieces and nephews living in dear old Madison-The Gibsons.

William Hardenbrook.

WILLIAM HARPST
1837 - 1931

First Sergeant W. F. Harpst.
Company C.

William F. Harpst served in the 150th Regiment, Pennsylvania Volunteers during the Civil War. He also contributed material for the book, *150th Regiment, Pennsylvania Volunteers* by Lt. Colonel Thomas Chamberline, published in 1895, revised and reprinted in 1905.

Four companies initially mustered into the 150th from Crawford County, Pennsylvania. Most of the "recruits" were from Meadville. William F. Harpst bore a strong resemblance to Captain John Burris Fay, his half-brother.

His obituary appeared in the Meadville *Tribune Republican*:

Captain William F. Harpst, one of the oldest Civil War veterans in Mercer County, being in his 95th year, died Saturday afternoon at his home in Greenville after a long period of invalidism. Captain Harpst was born at Bellefonte, Centre County, Pa., in July 1837, and when an infant was brought to Meadville by his parents, the late Philip and Sarah Harpst. At the age of 14 he entered the office of the Cussewago Chronicle, a weekly paper, to learn the trade of a printer. At the age of 24 he enlisted as a union soldier, and remained in the service until the close of the war in the Spring of 1865. He resumed his work along the newspaper lines, and finally located at Greenville, being connected with the Argus, a weekly newspaper, and the year 1877 started the Daily Progress, a Democratic newspaper, which finally became a weekly publication, which he edited for many years. Captain Harpst has held the office of Jury Commissioner. He was a prominent in military matters for a long time, being interested in all that pertained to the welfare of the Grand Army of the Republic and kindred organizations. Surviving are his second wife and three daughters: Dr. Blanche Harpst, Duquesne, Pa., and Mrs. Alice Norosely and Mrs. Grace Hepfinger, both of Cleveland; also one brother, Frank Harpst, of Meadville. Among other surviving relatives is a niece, Mrs. John A. Yocum; Catherine Street, this City. Funeral from the home at 2 o'clock Tuesday afternoon. Interment in the Shenango Valley Cemetery. Died Sept. 26, 1931. Meadville Tribune Republican Sept. 28, 1931.

Martin Marshall Harry
1844 - 1918

Martin Marshall Harry enlisted in Company I, 16th Regiment, Illinois Volunteer Cavalry at Urbana, Illinois on December 26, 1862. He was enrolled for three years of service at Springfield, Illinois on January 21, 1863. He served under the command of Captain Jackson of Kankakee and entered action in Kentucky. On one of the scouting raids made by his regiment through Lee County, Virginia he and 185 of his comrades were captured by the Confederate Army. He was sent to Lynchburg, Virginia and then on to Richmond and spent two months in the prison camp at Belle Isle in the James River. From there he was sent to Andersonville, for over eleven months and in that notorious stockade suffered everything that a human being could be called on to endure. From Andersonville he was removed to Florence, South Carolina because Sherman's army was rapidly advancing across the Carolinas. Finally the order came to exchange 10,000 sick and convalescent prisoners, and they were paroled at Benton Barracks in St. Louis. He was moved frequently until finally mustered out at Nashville, Tennessee on August 19, 1865. During his service he was promoted to Sergeant.

Martin and his brother

Martin Marshall was born January 8, 1844 in Lewis County, Kentucky. He was the oldest of seven children born to Joseph and Lucinda "Ruggles" Harry. He died October 3, 1918 in Urbana, Champaign County, Illinois and is buried at Mt. Olive Cemetery, Mayview, Champaign, Illinois. He married Olivine "Dilling" Harry on January 9, 1868 and they had two children. Olivine died in 1873. On October 21, 1877, Martin married Mary Jemima "Boyd" Harry and they had four children.

MILTON HEPLER
1843 - 1919

Milton Hepler was born January 12, 1843, on the farm of his parents, Jacob and Mary Brinker Hepler. There he spent the first twenty one years of his life, attending district school and working for his father on the farm. He married Margaret Jane Bolton. In February 1864, he enlisted for service in Company K, 14th Pennsylvania Cavalry, commanded by Colonel Schoonmaker. He was examined at Meadville and taken to Camp Copeland at Pittsburgh, where he became partially hardened for service by sleeping on muddy fields for three weeks. The next move was to Martinsburg, West Virginia, where he came near dying of the mumps. The 14th Cavalry started up the Shenandoah Valley through Winchester and encountered the Rebels in the battle of Piedmont.

Milton told his daughter about his wartime experiences which she recorded:

This was my first real experience of war. We were commanded by Gen. Sigel and were defeated. We went into camp in the woods about nine o'clock at night. The rebels were there to receive us and their greeting was very warm. They showered us with bullets while the heavens showered us with a drenching rain. We fought blindly but desperately in the dark and succeeded in repulsing the enemy. The rain continued throughout the night. The enemy had received 8,000 reinforcements and just as we were boiling our coffee for dinner a shell fell in the camp. We deserted our coffee, drew up into battle line and fought for four hours. At that time I was with Battery B, U.S. Artillery. The rebs came in with a flank movement; Gen. Sigel rode up and listlessly called out, "Fight a little, boys, fight a little." In a short time he rode up again and ordered us to get out. We were surrounded by yelling rebels but managed to escape in the confusion. Just then, Gen. Sigel was shot in the arm; it fell to his side and he galloped away in the rain. I could see our infantry rushing down the hillside with the rebels in hot pursuit. They drove us back to Cedar Creek where we remained unmolested for five or six days recruiting our forces. It was four days before the stragglers returned from the mountains. Crawling through bushes and among the rocks some came in almost naked.

Gen. Hunter relieved Gen. Sigel at Cedar Creek and we started up the Shenandoah Valley again. We crossed the stream at New Market and camped for the night. The next day was Sunday; we were ordered out and marched about half a mile. The enemy had built breastworks and advanced. They surprised us, repulsed our cavalry and almost captured our artillery. Concentrating our forces the cavalry and infantry drove them back to their breastworks where they made a stand. Our cavalry charged and the artillery followed, but the enemy had 36 pieces of artillery ready for us. We were repulsed, but re-assembled our own 36

MILTON HEPLER
1843 - 1919

pieces of artillery and with our cavalry we again advanced within twenty rods of the breastworks of rails, logs, and stumps. Our shells and solid shot against the treacherous breastworks hurled pieces of rails and logs into the enemy's lines and killed more of their men than did the bullets of our muskets. The rails took fire and fell among the wounded and dying. Many who would have recovered from wounds were roasted alive. That morning 100 cadets came out from Lexington in their sleek uniforms and joined the rebel ranks. Many of them were wounded at the breastworks and burned alive—a beautiful sacrifice to the lost cause. The enemy, finding they could not withstand our fire, hastily retreated. Our cavalry dismounted and advanced; then we charged, capturing 1200 men and killing Gen. Miles, the rebel commander, in the woods.

Milton Hepler & Family

Going over the battlefield with a comrade, I saw heads of many boys, lying five feet from their bodies. Many were disemboweled; signs of life were still evident in the shattered bodies. Others were burned to a crisp where they fell beside the breastworks. We came across one man with both legs broken; he had crept a quarter of a mile, dragging his musket with him. When we approached him, he was so filled with bitterness and hatred that he tried to shoot us.

We gathered up the wounded and left them in an old house under a white flag.

We came upon the enemy at Staunton and followed them to Lynchburg where we engaged them and defeated them. They received re-enforcements by rail from Richmond and four times they tried to break our center but we held our ground and fought until after dark. Then Gen. Hunter, seeing we were outnumbered, prepared to retreat. Leaving our campfires burning, we stole away in the night and marched ten miles before the rebels knew of our departure. For some time we had been annoyed by bushwhackers who continued to pick off our men. We went after them and captured thirty of their number. Our rations were running low and we subsisted for several days in the mountains on birch bark and clover tops. When we found a cow, we would run a saber through her neck, cut a piece from her body and carry it, warm and dripping with blood, until we found an opportunity to cook it. Occasionally we picked up a few hoe cakes at a farm house, for these the officers offered $5.00 apiece. We succeeded in getting word through to Charleston that the army was starving and a wagon train was sent to meet us. We came up with the wagon train about 50 miles from Charleston, after having marched and fought for 42 days on 12 days rations. We continued to Charleston where we remained a week recruiting our strength and weakly endeavoring

MILTON HEPLER
1843 - 1919

to exterminate the greybacks, another enemy of our army. I went into the mill dam to wash my clothes and was caught in the swirl of water and carried beyond my depth. I could not swim a stroke; twice I went down, and coming up called for help. My comrades on the shore saw me but thought I was diving and made no effort to save me. The last time I could make no outcry but my wild efforts brought aid. A comrade dived for me, found me and dragged me to shore, where after strenuous efforts to resuscitate me, I was brought back to life.

We moved to Parkersburg for a few days. Later came the Battle of Winchester. We went into the battle at four o'clock in the morning with 80,000 men. The rebels had the same number. The fighting was terrific. We were forced to gather up the bodies of our men to make way for our artillery. I found a large shepherd dog guarding the lifeless body of his master. We were defeated in the morning, but regained the battle in the afternoon about four o'clock. Our victory was due to Sheridan's famous charge through a gap in the breastworks. He won the battle by having the cavalry use carbines instead of the saber as the rebels expected. In this battle we lost 6,500 and the enemy 5,500. Three days later, September 22, 1864, we were called out at daybreak and marched to Strasburg where we encountered the enemy on the hill, fortified in two lines of breastworks. We forded the stream and Sheridan, by a circuitous route of eleven miles, repeated his unique charge of the previous battle and in like manner defeated the enemy. We won the battle in the evening. The enemy lost 6,000 and we lost 5,000 in this battle. We drove Gen. Early up the valley and over the natural bridge. We had orders to burn every barn containing hay or straw and take all cattle and chickens. Gen. Early took advantage of Sheridan's absence and stealing in before daylight, attacked the Eight Corps and routed them. They were so greatly surprised that they fled pell-mell without shoes or clothing. Sheridan, twenty miles away, heard the firing and started at once for the scene of the battle. He met the panic stricken soldiers and said "Turn, boys, turn. We're going back." Sheridan rode up again to us about four o'clock in the evening and said, "Boys, we will camp tonight on the old camp grounds, cheer up." And we did. Then we drove the rebels before us for four days. We returned to Winchester and went into camp. We remained there in temporary winter quarters and skirmished over a radius of forty miles. One night we captured a colonel, a medical director and five privates, who were attending a party. Returning with them I was thrown from my horse while fording a stream filled with floating ice.

MILTON HEPLER
1843 - 1919

The next spring we went up of the valley again; this time under Hancock, and made a clean sweep of everything up to the time of Lee's surrender. We went to Washington for the grand review and were then ordered to Fort Leavenworth, Kansas. We returned to Pittsburgh and were mustered out September, 1865. I then returned to Clarion County, settled down, bought a farm and have resided there over since.

Milton wrote a few letters home and to his Mother and brother who was also in the Union Army:

Camp _____ Western Virginia January 20th 1865:
Dear mother,
I seat myself this morning to write a few lines to let you know I am still numbered among the
living and I am well and hardy yet. Not knowing how long it may last but I thank god that he has spared me so far through danger and I trust that he will spare me through all danger wherever I may be.

Dear mother,
I suppose you have heard of the death of P.K. Hamm. We lifted him yesterday and fetched him to Winchester and got him put him (in) a coffin and his body starts for home this morning. I suppose you will go to see buried (see him buried?). We sent him home in the best style
we could. William McNutt tried his best to send him home right away but he couldn't get him sent. He was a good soldier. Many pleasant hours we all spent around our little campfire in talking and singing. William McNutt is well. Him and I are the only two left out of 7 that was together last spring. Robert McNutt is sick and is in the hospital. Lieutenant McNutt is lay sick in the hospital with typhoid fever. He is pretty bad with it. I suppose when the draft comes of it will more likely give brother Henry a call. That will be sad for him if he as to come but I trust that he may escape the draft this time. I expect Thomas will be exept from the draft. Mother I'm very glad that I enlisted when I did and have almost a year in and if I hadn't enlisted then I might have been home yet and in great trouble about the draft but so I am here now and know what soldiering is. It is a very hard life to endure not knowing what moment we may rush right in to danger. We must look to god for our deliverance. He is our only friend that we can trust for our course. Dear mother I must bring my letter to a close for this time. Here mother I will send you a present. So goodbye for this time.

Your affection (affectionate)
son, Milton Hepler.

This is a letter Milton wrote to his brother.
Camp near Halltown
April 10th, 1865

Milton Hepler
1843 - 1919

Dear Brother

I received your welcome letter a few days ago. I was glad to hear that you are all well. I am well and harty. I wold of rote to you sooner but we are move a round so mutch that I haven't time to rite. There was a salute fired today at Winchester of 200 canon shots for the capture of General Lee and his army. I think this war will soon play out. I don't think that the men that were drafted will git to see any wild rebs at tall. Everything looks verry favorable on our side now. I hant time to rite mutch this time and I hev a verry poor place to rite. It is verry disagreeable day. It is raining. It rained all last night. I was on picket. It was verry disagreeable night. Please rite soon and tell me all the names of the drafted men that had to go.

So good by fo this time
Yours
Milton Hepler
Harpers Ferry, VA 14 Pa CA Co K
Rite soon

Burn this letter

Milton became a member of the Captain Core Post No. 239 of the G.A.R. During the war Milton's older brother Thomas served in the early part of the war losing a leg at the battle of Stone River, Murfreesboro, Tennessee he was a member of the 78th Pennsylvania Volunteers. Milton Hepler died in 1919.

Thomas Hepler
1837-1904

Thomas Hepler born in Clarion County, Pennsylvania, the son of Jacob and Mary Brinker Hepler. He served in the 78th Pennsylvana Infantry during the Civil War losing a leg after the battle of Stone River in Murfreesboro, Tennessee on December 31, 1862. This is a letter written to Thomas from his brother Benjamin Hepler:

Drywood Vernon Co., MO
March 3, 1862

Thomas Hepler
78 Reg. PA Volunteer

My verry dear brother,
I was never more surprised than I was last evening (on my return to my dear family after an absence of 2 days on professional duty) to receive a letter from you bearing date of 6th (apr ?) stating that you was engaged in

Thomas Hepler
1837-1904

common with many of my own cousins and old and loved friends in prosecuting a war of persecution and extermination. Now this is the rub. If I thought you were doing as I have charged you with abolition sentiments I would stop writing this moment but I allow myself to hope that you are battling for the union and the constitution and equal rights. I can meet you as a friend and brother on the same cause. I have belonged to a military organization for the last 15 months better to protect law and order during last summer our counties on the border were over run with outlaws from Kansas belonging to no military command robbing every family that would express sympathy with the south and occasionally would kill persons of note. My life was threatened by many about the first of last September. Maj Gen Price return from Springfield after gaining the battle there and fought a small force commanded by Gen Lane within 8 miles of where I live. I was in the battle. It only lasted one hour when the government troops fled. The loss on the part of the rebels was 2 kill and 22 wounded 4 of which I tended on my self and they have all recovered. After this battle I was appointed Surgeon of the 7 Cavl Regiment. I served 2 months as regiment surgeon when I was promoted to Division Surgeon at the hospital at Cassville where I remained to the 25th of Nov. At which time I discharged the most of my invalids and left the balance in charge of my assistant and on my way in returning to the main body of the army I fell into the hands of the government troops who arrested my and took me as a prisoner of war to Fort Scott Kansas where they released me on parole when I returned home to my family and found them all well but almost destitute of everything else. Our farm consisting of 50 acres under fence and cultivation was entirely destroyed by fire burning up all my hay and some corn. I had a fine crop of corn here and on an other farm in all 75 or 6 acres but when Gen Lane passed through this country he campt within ½ mile of my house and he had need of all _____ corn as it did not cost anything. He also took all the pork hogs that I had. Previous to his coming along the Kansas Jayhawkers robbed our house 5 different times taking all my papers, notes and _____ and furs. Some ____ clothing Sarah's jewelry a fine carriage and horse and all my clothing and about 40 or 50 dollars worth of medicine. They have since give back the horse and Sarah's jewelry but they have not given back nor paid for anything else they have taken. My cost and damage since last May well exceed $3000 besides enduring more hardships during the last 6 months then I ever did or expect to again as I could not endure it six months longer. My letter is getting tolerable lengthy but as it is very uncertain when I will have an opportunity of addressing you again I will fill up another sheet. Not withstanding all my misfortunes I feel that I am ____ ____ and will contend for right and justice. I have a good many warm friends and I exercise some influence and can make a comfortable living if I were to loose all I had and ½ what I make in my profession. I have been unusually successful during this last 18 month. In fact I am compelled to refuse practice nearly every day owing to the press of businesses I have on hand. Our diseases this winter have been of the most violent character principally pneumonia and typhoid fever of which I have not lost but one patient. I have now 4 cases of typhoid fever under treatment 18 miles from home and they are all likely to recover. My health has been unusually good ever since I came west until lately I

Thomas Hepler
1837-1904

have been threatened with typhoid fever but I think with care I will avoid an attack of it. My family consists of my dear wife and 3 little children 2 girls and one boy all in excellent health. Mary Jane can spell and will soon learn to read. If this communication should reach you enjoying similar health to what you did at the time you wrote to me you will then take into consideration the advice I here with submit to you knowing the exposed conditions of a soldiers life I can advise you from experience. When on picket or extra duty no matter how tired or sleepy you are never lye down on the cold damp ground to rest or sleep until you are dry and warm and you have made down a bed with straw or leaves or hay or blankets or something sufficient to keep your body from being exposed to the damp earth. Eat as regular as possible and when you are from necessity compelled to do without food or water any length of time be verry careful and avoid excess when you obtain it. Avoid cooling off suddenly when you are verry warm. Don't waste your money and endanger your health by buying luxuries and confectionaries and eating at irregular periods but rather save your dimes should you at any time get wounded or fall a victim to disease. Then you will find use for your loose change in procuring a little extra nursing and some little dainties and

luxuries that are indispensable to a sick man and if no account to a well one. In time of battle lay down and draw a dead man over you until the fight is over oh no no you must recollect that you have volunteered what for, to obey all orders from your superior officers and that to from the old Key Stone State. Never, never disgrace your company your state nor country but battle manfully for the cause you espouse but be considerate don't rush into danger and commit suicide nor hide to take some secret advantage of the foe and there by commit murder. You doubtless know that your foe are men like your self neither brutes nor gods but simply American people and many good and brave men pray to god that they may be peace made you restored to your kind friends at home without the shedding of any more blood in this unjust and unholy war. Direct your letters to Fort Scott, Kansas.

Unsigned
(from brother Benjamin Hepler)

This is a letter from Thomas to his sister:
Murfreesboro
February 10th/63

Dear Sister

Being I am at leisure on my bunk in the hospital at Murfreesboro, I thought it my duty as a brother to write unto you in order to make you acquainted with my case. Well I am getting along as well as can be expected under existing circumstances but my wound still gives me some pain. The wound itself is filling up fast but there appears to be some irritation existing close to the wound which is occasioned only the bone being injured but hope that difficulty will soon be removed by proper care and attention. Otherwise I feel well. I have a good appetite and all victuals appear to agree with me. All the rest of our wounded......
...being healthy also our Reg't except the Colonel he is not as well as he might be but hoping he will again regain his health. You have no

Thomas Hepler
1837-1904

doubt already heard and read a full detail of the battle before Murfreesboro, I do therefore not deem it necessary to say any more about it but I must say that our Reg't gained for itself and the Keystone State that send it a name which will be recorded on the pages of history which will long be remembered by all those who may deem it fit to read. There is nothing new at present, all things appear to be quiet only I think preparations are being made for another move. It appears the rebels are at ....fight the boys are eager for a pitch in. We think success will be our lot especially in the cause we are engaged in. I put it down as a true maxim that our side of the question is just and right and therefore need not fear. I must also state to you that I was taken prisoner and paroled and my case being considered rather severe they did not take me along with them but left me in Murfreesboro and when our men took possession of the town I again fell into the hands of our men and am will cared for and hope I will soon be able to be about again. I received a letter from brother Henry about one week ago and I answered it. I understood by Henry's letter that you received the money.....

I will now close by asking you to give me some information concerning the immortal renowned brave and chivalries Capt J. M. Brinker. We have heard of some of his great and daring exploits he performed during his sojourn among you. I for my part think it would be far better policy for him to be with his men. We are now entirely destitute of a commander but he is not gentleman enough to be among his men. I can assure you he is very little thought of by his men and he will find it so whenever he joins his company. Please leave me know what he is thought of and write soon. Your cousin Sam'l Hepler is well and doing well.

No more but remain your Brother

Thomas Hepler

Thomas Hepler died in 1904.

Jacob Hess
1837 - 1896

Jacob Hess was born in 1837, the son of James Hess (born 1810 in Germany) and Permia Cooper (born 1820 in Pennsylvania). Jacob's siblings were: Scott born 1838, Jeremiah born 1839, Rolla born 1844, William born 1846, and James born 1848. According to the family bible, the Hess children were all born in Scioto-Leo, Ohio. This is also verified in the 1850 Ohio Census. This census lists a John Hess born 1826 in Germany, in the same household. They were christened German Methodist. Jacob Hess married Amanda Eleanor York, who was born in Terra Haute, Indiana. Before the war Jacob was a farmer.

Jacob Hess joined the 119th Illinois Volunteers, Company G. On December 21, 1862. In Tennessee, Jacob was taken prisoner with his whole company at Rutherford Station. Jacob was released from prison and he joined the 15th Regiment Veteran Reserve, Company A, on the 12th of August 1862. On the 13th of July 1865 he was discharged by General Order 116.

Ashbel Fairchild Hill
1842 - 1876

A.F. Hill was born to James and Martha Kefover Hill on October 23, 1842 in German Township, Fayette County, Pennsylvania. Even as a young boy he was inclined to create stories and poems that would delight family and friends. As a young lad he clerked in a small store in Smithfield, Pennsylvania owned by Captain McCleary. There he witnessed at a summer celebration a fight between some boys of the town and a produce vendor and penned a poem called the "Watermelon Riot," at age 16, it became his first published article.

When the War Between the States began he responded to the call of his country for volunteers early in 1861 and enlisted as a member of Company D raised in Fayette County, Pennsylvania by Captain C.L. Conner. Attached to the Eighth Regiment of the Pennsylvania Reserves, commanded by Colonel Hays; afterwards Oliphant and Bailey he was mustered in as a private, June 21, 1861 and promoted to Sergeant May 1, 1862. He participated in the engagements in Manassas, Bull Run, Hunter's Mills, Mechanicville, Gaines' Mill, and the battles of the Chickahominy, South Mountain and Antietam. At the latter he lost a leg and lay at the edge of the Cornfield. He was discharged from the army by Surgeon's certificate in December 1862.

A.F. Hill was a fine scholar and at one time editor of the *Golden City* in San Francisco, assistant editor of the *Philadelphia Mercury*, and was a contributor to *Saturday Night* and other literary papers. He was the author of several widely read publications, the most popular being: "White Rocks," a true story of the murder of Polly Williams a young girl thrown to her death by her lover, that took place in Fayette County, Pennsylvania in 1811. "Our Boys" a history from the soldiers perspective of the boys of the Eighth Pennsylvania Reserves. The editor sued, "Secrets Of The Sanctum," a tale of power and distrust of the editor of a Philadelphia Newspaper. "John Smith's Funny Adventure on a Crutch," the life of a young soldier who lost a leg during the Civil War, traveling around the country, and a serial published in the *Genius of Liberty*, "Able Gray or Romance on the National Road." During his time in San Francisco he met and married a young lady named Mary. In 1874 he returned to Fayette County, Pennsylvania and immediately began writing for the *Genius of Liberty*.

Not long after his return he and Mary divorced in 1875 and she returned to California. On October 28, 1876 he delivered an address at New Geneva during a drizzling rain and his clothing became wet and in this condition he returned to Uniontown, Pennsylvania a distance of fifteen miles to the McClell House where he had been residing. A severe cold resulted, followed by fever and although he had the best medical attention, his system never recovered from the severe attack and he passed quietly away on November 7, 1876 at age 34. His remains were taken to Masontown, Pennsylvania on November 8, and buried the following day.

Issac Hillkirk
1838 -

Issac Hillkirk was born on December 31, 1838 in Hickory Township, Mercer County, Pennsylvania. He married Minerva Buchanan on June 23, 1863 and they had nine children. Prior to his enlistment Isaac worked as a blacksmith. Issac joined the 39th Pennsylvania Volunteers, Company B, as a private on June 19th 1861. He was discharged for disability on February 15, 1863. Then on January 2, 1864 he enlisted as a private with the 101st Pennsylvania, Company C.

Isaac was listed as a prisoner of war on April 20th 1864. During the war Isaac re-enlisted a second time so that a fellow soldier could be home with his sick wife, it was during this time Isaac was captured and became a prisoner at Andersonville. On February 18, 1865, a Dr. Kugler wrote that Issac suffered from rheumatism and scurvy along with breast pain and a severe cough and requested a 20-day extension of his furlough that was to have ended on February 23rd. On March 15, 1865 Isaac saw yet another physician who said he was suffering from the same thing that Dr. Kugler diagnosed and it was the opinion of this physician that Isaac was unfit for duty and it was not safe for him to travel. He was mustered out on June 25, 1865 at New Bern, North Carolina.

His pension request, dated April 28, 1881, stated he was disabled by diarrhea and scurvy while a prisoner of war and contained several letters of testimony from employers, neighbors and acquaintances. His employer of fifteen years wrote, "I have known him to be so afflicted with rheumatism that he would have to quit work and go home and be confined in his bed for two weeks at a time. This occurred frequently. I do not consider him able to perform any manual labor though he tries to do some work. I do not think him able to do more work than a person having lost an arm or a leg."

Rev. Nicholas Holmes
1841 - 1915

Nicholas Howell Holmes was born in Denmark, December 29, 1841 and came to America in 1858, locating in Chautauqua County, New York. When Lincoln made his second call for troops to fight in the war Nicholas volunteered for service with the 1st Battalion, New York Sharpshooters, 7th Company as a corporal. This unit was organized by consolidation of the 6th Company Sharpshooters (who were originally organized at Rochester, New York on September 13, 1862) and the 7th Company (organized at Jamestown on September 12, 1862).

His unit participated in: the Siege of Suffolk, Bristoe campaign, Advance line of the Rappahannock, Mine Run, the Rapidan, Wilderness, Spotsylvania, assault on the salient "bloody angle," North Anna, Totopotomoy, Petersburg, Weldon Railroad, Boydton Plank Road, Dabney`s Mill, White Oak Road, Five Forks, Petersburg, and Appomattox Court House. In 1864 Nicholas Holmes was captured by Confederates and taken to Libby Prison then to Belle Island and finally to Salisbury where he escaped wearing a Confederate uniform. He walked the entire distance to the Union lines at the Ohio River where he arrived in time to vote for Lincoln in the presidential election.

Nicholas Holmes was present at the surrender of Robert E Lee's army in 1865. The loss for his battalion were 23 enlisted men killed and mortally wounded; and 1 officer and 38 enlisted men by disease, the total loss were 62 men. After the war Nicholas Holmes married Effie Angeline Gleason in 1873, she died in 1902, and he then married Mrs. Lillian Crawford. Nicholas received his license to preach in 1870 and graduated from Allegheny College and became a licensed member of the Erie Conference in 1879. Rev. Nicholas Holmes died in Washington D.C. in 1915 and is buried in Conneautville Cemetery.

WILLIAM WESLEY HUFFMAN
1845 - 1917

William Wesley Huffman (Bill) son of Henry Huffman married Livina Matilda Brown. Her father was a doctor, it was said that Dr. Brown went down to the river parked his horse and buggy got on a raft and was never heard of since. Some say he drowned. Her mother was Mary Ann (Courson) Hetrick who lived to the age of 96. She was living with William and Livina when she died. On the night Mary died Livina was singing a hymn to her, Bill was upstairs sleeping and was awaken and came down stairs to find her dead. He closed her eyes and told them to go to bed.

William and Lavina & family

William served as a private in Company B, 206th Regiment. This regiment was organized at Camp Reynolds, Pittsburg, Pennsylvania on September 8, 1864 under Colonel Hugh J. Brady and assigned to the Army of the James. On the 4th of October while engaged in building a fort near Dutch Gap, it was under the enemy's guns and had one man killed and several wounded. General Ord was put in command of the Army of the James. On the 26th of April 1865, as no further service being required it was sent to Pittsburg and was mustered out June 2,1865. General Dandy in command said of this regiment; "Under your gallant commander Col. Hugh Brady, you were the first to enter Richmond, and to display in the capital of traitors the Stars and Stripes of your country. Carry home with you and bequeath it to your children, The RED HEART, the badge of the first division. It is the symbol that will live when the present and succeeding generations have passed away."

William was said to have helped to release Union soldiers on a raid of a Andersonville Prison. How William met Livina is unknown, but they came from Jefferson County, from his father's farm or nearby area of Worthville or Coolsprings to the Charles Fisher farm and setup housekeeping near McWilliams Township, Armstrong County, Pennsylvania. He worked for Mr. Fisher on the farm until he bought his own farm, 217 acres at 50 cents a acre, on top of Mudlic Hill, Armstrong County, Pennsylvania.

William was a farmer in the summer and a lumberman in the winter. On his farm they cleared the land that was very stony and made stone fences around the fields. Later he traded his farm for his sons Dave's farm down in Mudlic and later sold this farm to another son Al. He then bought a house in Upper Mudlic up the road from Al's farm. This house is where he died years later of a stroke. William sold his lumber to Andrews Lumber Company in New Bethlehem, Pennsylvania and used the Red Bank Creek to float logs to the mill. When William's son John died at age 31 from a log falling on him William and Lavina raised John's three sons: Erwin (Windy), William, and Homer. John's wife was said to have gone either to Florida or Rensoldsville, Pennsylvania.

WILLIAM WESLEY HUFFMAN
1845 - 1917

William had a white beard in later life, he chewed tobacco and was said to have a temper. On his deathbed he laid for two weeks with out being able to talk and it was difficult for him to swallow. The grandchildren came to see him and marched around his bed. They would read the bible to him. William died of a stroke, his son Dave died of a stroke in which he could not talk and yet later Dave's son Ernest (Jake) had a stroke in which he could not talk but lasted many years probably because of modern medicine.

JAMES HUNTER
1841 - 1923

James Hunter before the war was a farmer. He was one of the first to enlist with the 83rd Pennsylvania Volunteers, Company G on August 19, 1861. At the second battle of Bull Run, James was shot in the shoulder. James re-enlisted with the 18th Veteran Reserve, Company A. He mustered out of service on August 30, 1864.

The following obituary appeared in the *Forest Press*:

> *James Hunter, one of the oldest and most respected residents of Hickory Township, passed away at 6:33 o' clock Saturday morning, November 3, 1923 at his home in Endeavor, aged 82 years six months and 18 days. Although in failing health for sometime Mr. Hunter had been able to be about until a few days before his death, which was due to ailments incident to old age. Mr. Hunter was one of five sons and five daughters born to Samuel and Mary Hunter, original settlers on what is known as the Hunter place at Oldtown, later the location of the sawmill of the Coleman, Harter and McCormick Co. the Hunter family came to this section from Westmoreland county, settling first in Clarion county and clearing up the farm now known as the Bowman farm near Newmansville, from their they came to the farm at Oldtown, where the subject of this sketch was born April 15, 1841, and where he was reared to young manhood. This farm was sold during the early oil excitement and Mr. Hunter's family moved to a farm near Jamestown Mercer County Pennsylvania, James HUNTER served his country faithfully and well for three years during the civil war. Being one of the first 61 men who enlisted in Tionesta as members of company G, 83rd Pennsylvania Volunteers, they left Tionesta by flat boat on August 20 1861, being towed to Irvineton by William Halls team of horses, from their going to Erie by train, only four of the men of this original enlistment in company G are known to survive, as follows; D. W. CLARK of Tionesta, William Albaugh, of Albaugh Hill; John B*

James Hunter
1841 - 1923

McClatchy, of Union city Pa, and Rev. J Boyd Leedom, of Los Angeles California. Mr. Hunter was seriously wounded in the second battle of Bull Run, a rifle ball passing through his left shoulder, which left him a cripple for the remainder of his life, he continued in the service after his recovery, serving the full term of his enlistment and receiving an honorable discharge. At Stowtown, now Endeavor, in December1864 Mr. Hunter was united in marriage with Miss Martha Elizabeth Hillard, who was born at Hillard Station, Butler county Pa September 10 1844, to them were born six children, five of whom, with the mother survive as follows; Mrs. Robert McMillan, Samuel Hunter, Burr Hunter and Mrs. Carl Range, all of Endeavor, Guy Hunter, of East Hickory, Mr. Hunter is also survived by one brother and two sisters, as follows, John Hunter of Ross Run; Mrs. Mary Angles, Kinsman Ohio and Mrs. Carrie Erdice of Jamestown ,Pa. Mr. Hunter cleared up the farm now owned by his son Burr Hunter ,in Beaver Valley ,and it was one of the best in that section. He was employed in the lumber woods by the late T. D. Collins and for the past forty years had been in the employ of the Wheeler and Dusenbury Company, for thirty five years he had been a consistent member of the Free Methodist Church and was esteemed by all who bore his acquaintances a Christian gentleman in every sense of the word. Funeral services in his memory were held at one o'clock Monday afternoon in the Townline Free Methodist Church, Rev., G. S. Bryan of Warren Officiating, assisted by Rev., A. H. M. Zahniser of Tionesta and Rev. Stimer of Tidioute. The aged veteran was given full military honors in his burial a detail from Gus E. Warden Post American Legion, of Endeavor furnishing the bearers of the pall and firing a salute of farewell over his grave. Interment was made in the Townline Cemetery.

Joseph Buffington Jackson
1845 - 1927

Joseph Buffington Jackson was born to John Jackson of Armstrong County and Elizabeth McCartney of Indiana County. He married Caroline McNary of Washington County, on June 26, 1873 in Cannonsburg, Pennsylvania. Caroline was the daughter of William McNary and Margaret Murry. Joseph came from a family of ten children and was one of five brothers to serve in the Civil War. One of Joseph's brothers was General Samuel McCartney Jackson. Their Grandfather was one of the original settlers in Kiskiminates Township.

Joseph Jackson joined the 2nd Battalion, Pennsylvania Volunteer Infantry, Company D and served from 1863 until 1864, as a private, he mustered out with his company on January 21, 1864.

After the war, Joseph became a Presbyterian minister and served at several United Presbyterian Churches in Nebraska and Iowa.

BENJAMIN JOHNSON
1836 - 1875

In 1860 he was a 24 year-old farmer in Center Township, Greene County, Missouri with a wife and two young sons, ages 2 and 1. On June 22, 1861 he enlisted as a private in Company A, 3rd Missouri Infantry. The Battle of Wilson's Creek, August 11, 1861, occurred about 15 miles from his homestead on the day his mother was buried in John's Chapel Cemetery (a family member in later years said they could hear the guns). I am sure that his unit of the Missouri State Guard (McBride's Division) was involved in the battle. He was discharged December 11, 1861 and was paid $89.40 on April 28, 1862. His enlistment on August 1, 1862 in Captain A. Don Brown's Company, Greene's Regiment, Missouri Volunteers as a private at Rolling Prairie, Carroll County, Arkansas. He then appeared on the Company A, 3rd Regiment, Missouri Cavalry Muster Roll from August 1, to December 31, 1862, and is shown as "Transferred by promotion to Senior 2nd Lieutenant, Company "H" (Capt. James F. Wyatt's Company), Greene's Regiment (Col. Colton Greene) October 3, 1862 at Pocahontas, Arkansas."

The *Official Records of the War of the Rebellion* for his unit indicates that it was involved almost constantly in battles, skirmishes and raids in northern Arkansas and southern Missouri during 1863 and 1864. Lt. Colonel Leonidas C. Campbell, mustering officer wrote: " Detachments from this company ("H") were engaged in actions November 8, 1862 at Fort Stevenson, Douglas County, Missouri, December 4, 1862 near Hartville, Missouri, and December 24, 1862 near Van Buren, Missouri." In all of these actions they were victorious, and bore themselves gallantly. They have marched in various scouts and against the enemy 1,130 miles. They have been constantly on duty in front of the enemy on the border. This company is efficient in action, arms poor, private guns of various kinds, and no equipments (sic.). The property in its possession was mostly captured."

In January and February, 1864 the Company Muster Roll lists him as "Capt. Benjamin S. Johnson, Company "H", 3rd Regiment Missouri Cavalry at Jacksonport, Arkansas." On February 26, 1864 he was listed as "absent with leave." His wife and children had left Missouri during the war for safety probably during late 1862 or early 1863 and moved down into safer territory in Arkansas during General Sterling Price's last Missouri raid in the Fall of 1864. Captain Benjamin S. Johnson was promoted in the field by Colonel Colton Greene to command the 3rd Missouri Cavalry Regiment temporarily on October 23, 1864. Colonel Greene reported, "Here the injuries and wound received at Blue Mills the day before became so painful that I was compelled to turn my regiment over to Capt. B. S. Johnson, whose report of an action on the 23rd of October is herewith annexed, and to whom much commendation is due for uniform skill and courage while in command." Captain Johnson's subsequent report of the action appears in the *Official Records of the War of the Rebellion* as follows:

> *Report of Capt. Benjamin S. Johnson, Third Missouri Cavalry: CAMP ON RED RIVER ARK, December 8, 1864 MAJOR: I have the honor to make the following report of the part taken by this regiment in the action of the 23rd of October at Big Blue River: I assumed command of the regiment the evening of the 22nd of October, Colonel Greene being disabled from injuries received at the battle of Little Blue on the 21st of October. I was ordered to form the regiment at sunrise*

Benjamin Johnson
1836 - 1875

on the bank of Big Blue River as infantry. After being in position about half and hour the enemy appeared in sight and opened fire on us from small-arms, compelling us, owing to the formation of the creek, to leave our position, they being enabled to fire on us from the right flank and rear. We fell back one mile and a half in good order to a skirt of timber at the edge of a small prairie, and were ordered to form to support Pratt's artillery. The enemy appeared in sight and opened heavily upon us. We replied, compelling them to fall back to the shelter of some houses on the prairie. They again advanced at a charge to take our battery. We opened fire on them while Company G, under the command of First Sergeant Woolsey, dashed gallantly forward and hauled the guns off by hand, the balance of the regiment keeping a steady fire upon the enemy. We remained in our position until every gun was discharged and every cartridge expended. Ordered by General Clark to fall back to our horses, which we did in good order. Our loss was 3 killed and 7 wounded. The whole regiment acted very gallantly. Particular praise is due to Sergeant Woolsey, of Company G, for his gallant conduct. I am, major, very respectfully, your obedient servant, B. S. JOHNSON, Captain, Commanding Regiment. Maj. F. S. Robertson, Acting Assistant Adjutant-General, Marmaduke's Brigade.

The record also states that at the end of the war "...After a brief stay in Mexico, Greene returned to the U.S. and settled in Memphis, Tennessee. In partnership with other Missouri exiles, he started an insurance agency and in a remarkably short time rebuilt his fortune." It is not known if Benjamin S. Johnson went with Colonel Greene to Mexico or not, as others did with Colonel Jo Shelby to offer their services to Maximillian. It is known that he showed up in McKinney, Collin County, Texas a couple of years later. A November 1869 voter registration stated that he had lived in the county two years. According to his widow (who lived until 1914) the family stayed in Arkansas for some period of time before moving to Collin County, Texas. Captain Johnson's friend and former army surgeon in the 3rd Missouri Cavalry, Dr. Andrew Gullet, also settled in McKinney, Texas about the same time (1867) and became a prominent physician and member of the County Democratic Committee. I suspect that Dr. Gullet might have had some influence in his election (or appointment) as City Marshal of McKinney, Texas in 1872 or 1873. Unfortunately, the municipal records of the city of McKinney prior to 1881 have been lost. However, we have been able to confirm that he was City Marshal from an obituary notice in the *Dallas Daily Herald*, which mentioned his February 2, 1875 death as follows: "McKinney has lost its city marshal, Capt. Ben S. Johnson, one of "Pap" Price's veterans." Capt. Ben S. Johnson is buried in Pecan Grove Cemetery, McKinney, Texas near his friend, Dr. Andrew Gullet, who died in 1903. One of Ben's sons was named Andrew Gullet Johnson and was called "Doc" as a nickname.

DANIEL JONES
1835-1900

Daniel Jones, son of Daniel Jones and Martha Washington, served in the Civil War as a private in Company B, 57th Pennsylvania Volunteer Infantry, 2nd Division, 3rd Army Corp. He was captured and exchanged. He fought at Yorktown, Williamsburg, Peninsular Campaign, Seven Days' fight, Second Bull Run, Fredericksburg, Cold Harbor, Petersburg and others.

He married Mary Mollie Bowman (1846-1931). Daniel was part of the State of Pennsylvania. Militia as a Lieutenant in the Cooperstown Militia after service in the Civil War.

JESSE EVANS JONES
1840 - 1904

A native Pennsylvanian Jesse was born in Fayette County on January 22, 1840, the son of James and Anna Ross Jones. At the outbreak of the Civil War, he was engaged in farming, and was 22 years old when he enlisted from Woodbridgetown, Pennsylvania on September 22, 1861. He was as a private in Company G, 85th Pennsylvania Volunteer Infantry (also known as the Bloody 85th). In due time he was promoted to sergeant.

He married Lavina Bowers and had 2 children: Owen Morgan and Sarah Eliza Jones. When he left to join his regiment in Uniontown, Pennsylvania, he and his young wife parted ways at the sycamore tree crossroads, said their good-byes never to

Jesse Evans Jones
1840 - 1904

see each other again, she died of consumption while he was away at war, leaving their two young children to be raised by his Mother.

On August 14, 1864 he was wounded in the right hand at the battle of Deep Bottom, Virginia and taken to the hospital at Fortress Monroe, Virginia for three weeks then to Philadelphia for another three weeks. In September 1864 he was furloughed for thirty days, this was extended forty days and afterwards he returned to Morris Island. He took part in several decisive battles of the War: Fair Oaks, the seven days fight before Richmond, Whitehall, siege of Charleston and the siege of Richmond. He was honorably discharged at Pittsburg, Pennsylvania on November 22, 1864.

His brothers: Ralph, served in the 1st West Virginia Cavalry and Jerry served in Company G, 8th Pennsylvania Reserves. Jerry was wounded and captured at Weldon Railroad and taken to Salisbury Prison where died at the age of 22 and was buried in an unmarked grave. Their Grandfather, Able Jones, served in the Revolutionary War, at Valley Forge. Jesse Jones was a member of the Jerry Jones G.A.R. Post No. 541.

After the war he returned to Fayette County, Pennsylvania and married Sarah Davis. They had the following children: Jerry, Hannah, Almira, William, Lavina, Julia, Perie, James, John, Frances, Dora and Charles. He resumed the task of farming and later became a mail carrier, delivering mail in Smithfield, Pennsylvania and surrounding areas, in a small mail cart.

The following was taken from a Uniontown newspaper dated January 18, 1904:

Jerry Jones

> Stricken with paralysis after taking care of a small pox case, Smithfield Pennsylvania, Jesse Evans Jones, who took care of Wash Brown while he had the small pox, and up to the time of his death, had a paralytic stroke at the home of Mrs. Alice Brown, mother of Wash Brown (Alice was a sister to his first wife Lavina Bowers) he was then removed to his home in Rubles Mill, Pennsylvania, where he died on Sunday about 8 o'clock pm. He was buried in Mount Moriah cemetery, in Smithfield, Pennsylvania.

Jesse G. Jones
1842 -1917

Jesse was born in Sommerville, Morgan County, Alabama in 1842. He was orphaned by the age of fourteen in Mississippi. In 1856, he was adopted and educated by a businessman who saw potential in him even as a teenager. Jesse's sisters were raised in Alabama where they had previously lived. In February 1862 he enlisted in the Confederate Army, 7th Alabama Cavalry. He was 19 years of age when taken prisoner of war on February 16, 1862. This was the date when Fort Donaldson in western Tennessee was surrendered to the Union Army commanded by General Ulysses S. Grant. Grant insisted on "No terms except an unconditional and immediate surrender can be accepted." This battle and the "unconditional surrender" statement made Ulysses S. Grant a national hero. Jesse was one of about 13,000 troops stationed there. Although taken prison Jesse some how escaped through deep snow rather than being sent to the Chicago prisoner of war camps. According to his pension records he re-enlisted in the 28th Mississippi Cavalry, in Malone's Regiment. He was also wounded in the battle at Murfreesborro in the left elbow. The War Department's records stated that he enlisted as a private on the 14th of February 1864 in Fannin, Mississippi for a three-year period. Company muster rolls list him for March and April of 1865. His name appears on a roll of Prisoners of War, surrendered May 4, 1865, and paroled at Gainesville, Alabama, May 12, 1865.

Jesse was proud to have been a veteran of the Civil War and having fought for the South. During the war he carried the mail primarily as a cover for his spying activities for the Confederate Army. He was captured and escaped several times. He was wounded at Murfreesboro, but was not discharged until the 15th of May 1865 at Donville, Alabama.

The *Affidavit of Witness* signed by Richard F. Varnell, Jesse's brother-in-law, and dated, August 8, 1930 states: "I was raised in same community with Jesse Jones, husband of applicant, Mrs. Permelia Jones. I was about fifteen years of age at the time of his enlistment. I remember distinctly when he left home for Fort Donaldson and also remember of return home after the fall of Ft. Donaldson and his re-enlistment into Wheeler's Brigade. I also remember of his being at home on a furlough with a wounded arm. I can't say that I knew personally of the army service of Jesse Jones, but know that he visited home in the unniform(sic) and accoutrements of a confederate soldier."

Jesse wrote his reminisces between 1911-1912, at Knoxville, Texas:

Jesse G. Jones
1842 -1917

One of the most remarkable incidents of my Career in the army was my Capture by the federal Soldiers and escape in July 1862. Inexperience in warfare and only a 19-year-old boy limited as to generalship. I was face to face with the complex problem that went life or death to me. On the 16th of February Fort Donaldson was surrendered to the Federals. My regiment was included in the surrender, self excepted, who narrowly escaped by making a risky venture for liberty across the Cumberland river which was at that time swollen and angry. The snow was deep and the weather cold. The craft used for ferryboat would have been condemned for an ocean liner. About 20 happy souls rejoiced over their safe voyage and speedily disbanded into the woods which was rich in the verdure of thickets and colored my sympathy for the comrades left over in the Fort, for it was generally known that they were to go to Camp Douglas, Chicago. This rendered me almost heartbroken for I knew the biting cold of the climate would work sad havoc in their ranks. My own condition however required thought and much consideration for I was a long way from home, without friends, with a hostile force on my trial. My safety seems to lie in one direction only, that protection which the thickets offered. Yankee home guards patrolled the openings and roads thereby preventing my exit to more congenial parts. Hunger was not long in manifesting a morbid craving for food, to obtain which required risk, danger vigilance. The mandates of the appetite are absolutely monarchial and despotic. Perhaps there were ten or twelve houses in one mile of my headquarters; who they were and what they were, and to which side their sympathies belonged required a mind reader to foretell. The venture become urgent and had to be met regardless of consequences, and with the promptings of a famishing body with out further hesitancy I boldly appeared at the front door of one of these houses. "Madam," addressing the Lady at the door "my mission here is to confess the honor of being a Confederate soldier. I am driven by hunger to risk all and so far as I know may be digging my own grave; be that as it may, I have a few Yankee pennies I wish to invest in food." "Your Yankee shinplasters are despicable in my sight" she said "your gratitude for food is far more valuable to me. I have furnished the Confederacy my dear husband who is now famishing in prison," "Indeed kind Lady I feel fortunate that fate has directed my haphazard steps to your house. I feel imbued with new courage and greater loyalty for the kind words you have spoken, with one request now before parting and I will be up and going, Will any one of those houses in sight do to trust with my secret?" "One only, the one to the extreme right." "Thank you, thank you kindly, Good day." As I returned to the thicket my mental faculties were busy engaged in the solution of new ideas. Caution must be the watch word. All Generals great and small must have a begining the point was now reached to display my skill or else I was doomed to a horrid prisoner's fate. I first visited the loyal comrade pointed out by the kind Lady before maping a systomatic course. This gentleman proved to be well stocked with the information I most needed and desired and was fluently dispencing it to me when of a sudden we both was shocked and startled by the discovery of the house being surrounded with yankee soldiers. We both now was on the same footing. Sympathy for one another was all we had we knew and felt that our lot was desperate and our chances for escape very gloomy. The Bell Wood Iron works were located near the Cumberlan River 8 miles above Ft. Donalson and was in a scene of conflagration. The Confederates had used these works in the manufacture of Cannon for war. Wild consternation reigned with the Employers and all abbettors each supporing his sins the greatest as each had co-worked in the manufacture of war impliments for the Confederates. The old story of old dog Tray and his company was about to be demonstrated in my case. I was a Confederate Soldier and as such wonted to cast my lot. I had no proof nor witness to offer any acqusition the enemy pleased to make. Suspicion alone was all sufficient for cases of this kind under what charge whether that of a cannon maker or that of an escaped confederate Soldier mattered but little as my reward would be the same. The burning of Bell Wood furnices and the arrest of so many men created such a sensation that Confereate safety was under parr and if fortune did smile upon me and I was once more rewarded with a successful escape would have many things to promise myself, none however more to the

Jesse G. Jones
1842-1917

point than the old adage "Eternal Vigilance is the price of liberty." The Bell Wood prisoners proved up to be worse scared than hurt and was sent back home immediately, all except the head managers of the concern. As I did not belong to that class I got my freedom at the same time as the Subordinates. The charge of being an escaped confederate still hounded me and a small detail was on trial in the thickets in search of my whereabouts. I was making wonderful progress in learning with facts and tactics of war. I told my newly made friends good-bye wishing them all sorts of good luck and promising to return to them when the great excitement abated. I secluded my movements to the best of my skill and rambled away from the Fort. I felt my self too green to cope with Yankee army of two million soldiers with no better equipment for flank movements than my arsnal and cargo of war impliments presented. It was no longer a question with me of right. I had to assert my feble strength to produce might. My condition and attitude before the world required arms to defend myself. How to procure them was a hard problem. To request such ment a ready protest and ment a complete give away I determined to arise and get busy was in new fields of adventure enjoying the hospitality of a true blue Yankee Colonel. I drifted there knowing full well the confidence reposed in me. The Colonel was enthused over the brief rehersal given him and expressed great satisfaction in having the opportunity of paying a huge debt of gratitude due me prior to his Colonelcy he owned a farm near Fort Henry and had mowed quiet a quantity of hay. The Confederates going into winter quarters needed hay for beding the Colonel was spotted as a Union man and the hay was burned in the field. I had boarded with the Colonel in time was on chummy terms with him. Ten or twelve Confederates slyly approached his house one morning and made off with him to the woods with an inch rope around his neck leaving his wife and two grown daughters screaming and ringing their hands in the yard. They sought my services at once to interced for them and save the father and husband, my intersessions proved fruitless and these tuff characters were about to win the day when a etachment of cavalry per chance come to our relief and no doubt saved the life of this colonel my friend yet we are classed as enemies. Our gratitude for such can never die but liveth for ever. The Colonel plunged into details of my condition assuring me of his cheerfull help as I vowed secrecy in all he said or done consistance required that, life itself required it, for he had commited himself to my crimes, it would be embarrassing to him provided it was known. My advice was to return to the thickets and keep very quiet and await for every thing to still down, this seemed to be the only wise conclusion left me. War was at fever heat south east and west the territory completely covered with home guards. I did not want to fight anybody under existing circumstances. I wanted to get home at Corinth, Miss. and take a new start in warfare. To be captured here was too great a defeat to be tolerated by me, I wanted first to try my generalship and if necessary try my new arms which I had secured for my protection. I was quiet lonely in the thickets and started quickly at the breaking of a stick. I was supplied with rashions to run me a few days. Calm and tranquil seemed to be the outer world the chirping of birds and the barking of squirrels broke the monotony and tempered the lifeless world bearable. It may have been the best for me yo have been isolated from humanity for my protection and safety at that time, however, we trusted there was a limit. Day after day passed without developments and my patients was well nie exhausted, for a little recreation I thought I would visit the good lady's house who at first favored me with something to eat and posisbly may learn something beneficial to me. With a cautious step and alert I hastily approached her door inquiring if blue coats were plentifull in these parts. There is no scarsity to my sorrow, replied. Where were you when the furnices were burned and they carried of so many men? "I was also along with the crowd madam and sheared with them in their clemency. All of them were released at the Fort except a few head officers, yes you are correct my husband was one of them and was down there when you were here before, he is now at home where I trust he may remain, he is now coming from the barn and you may rely in him being all Southern." "Thank you, with your permission, speaking to the gentlemen I desire to introduce myself. "I am an escaped Confederate Soldier was in the Fort Donalson fight the command to which I belong were all captured and sent to camp Douglas Chicago." Giving me his hand remarked I am your friend, protecter, defender, and well wisher and will do your service when called. Under the present existing circumstances I have but little to do except watch and wait for the golden opportunity I want to keep up with the developments and friends, like you may aid me no little in

JESSE G. JONES
1842-1917

doing so. I do not wish to impose any trouble on others and would not have them to commit the crime of harboring me. Have you heard any hints either implied or expressed that would cause suspicion on the thickets being inhabited, reports are that is, slightly currant reports indicates one or more Confederates have been seen, as to the confederate I do not object to his company provided his company is good, if his escort is uniformed in blue I would hike away for parts unknown. There is one important matter on which your judgement and advise is respectfully asked, as you are familiar with the landscape surrounding here. Will you kindly point out to me every desirable hiding place, as I may be forced to move from point to point as occasions require. All of which was freely and unreservedly given. In conclusion beg you to try and keep wide a wake in the cause for the boys in gray. I hope that we may meet again, two long weeks have passed since I escaped and I am no nearer home. Thanking you kindly for your suggestions and advice bid you goodbye. Thinking perhaps that I was over doing caution and would do better to risk a little more, ventured out on the river to recconoit the country. I tried to be courteous to all I met and was like wise pleasantly greeted. Two Yankee Soldiers were repairing a telegraph line which had been destroyed. They swore vengance on the perpetrator if caught. My feeling was indescribable I rambled aimlessly on keeping the river for a land mark having a few words only with any body, though my head was crowded with thoughts of a plausable tale should I be detected. The Garrison left at the Fort had been changed so often indentifycation was not so seriously dreaded finding that I was inside of their picket line I sought out headquarters for the double purpose of gaining information and showing our respect. Gen. Oglesby twice Governor of Illinois was in command, his curtisies were faultless he inquired where I lived and if bothered by fleeing Confederates. I told him that I live out in the country, when I was sudently interupted by the acclimation, Spy Bushwhacker Telegraph distroyer from one of the Yankees who knew me. You are a gump exclaimed Gen. Ogelsby, very gumpy I will start you to camp Douglas tomorrow to join your people, off with him the Barracks. The sun was half an hour high when the prison door clanked behind me and I was left to my own reflections. I had much to stilmulate hope. Common sense war all sufficient to guide me on the only course practical, which was to make a risky venture to save or lose my life. This I would do regardless of consequences. As I was surveying the different departments I discovered a sick confederate soldier on a cot, "hello there, have you, too, been doing something naughty?" "I have been very sick for many days, unable to be moved when my regiment was sent to Camp Douglas.""What regiment was it? "it was the 26th Mississippi, my name is Reuben Tucker from Guntown and you are from Corinth?" Jesse Jones is my name and I am well acquainted with at least half of the 26th boys. Reuben I am glad to see and talk with you but very sorry to hear of your sickness and pained to know that you are a prisoner. "I am a prisoner also but have firmly decided not to remain one. I would rather die in the attempt for freedom than to rot away in a prison cell" "wait awhile friend before you undertake too rash a deed, circumstances govern matters of that kind and life is too precious and dear to haphazzard in speculation." "My case is too serious a one to admit of any delay which I have not the time now to give you in detail. I must commence my work after dark, or rather after the night officer has made his rounds. Positively I must refuse to listen to your pleadings to defer delay proceedings." "So determined a spirit invariably wins the victory, and if I was only stout enough to take care of myself would join you in the enterprise." "Oh no Reuben conditions are not alike, your army record is clean and clear, mine is debauched with every crime known to the foul deeds of humanity, that is why my case is so urgent my only defence to these foul charges is to elude arrest." "I understand your meaning" said Reuben. "The night officer will soon be around we had better get to our cots and feign to be asleep." so we did. The officer was satisfied that we were all O.K. and after he passed out I rolled off of my cot and told Reuben that I was going to make a careful search of the premises and would report to him before trying to escape. After careful inspection of the Baraicks wall I decided on a certain place being preferable to others. Though the sentinels were regularly distanced in their patrol or their beats, and any one wanting out must risk the marksmanship of a picket fifty yards distance, this I carefully weighed and accepted. Reuben begged to be heard on a very important matter. "It is true I am unwell but my courage is strong and I feel like I am capable of making an effort for my freedom. I want to go with you as far as the outside, then I think best to separate for fear that I might prove a burden to you. I came to this conclusion in the last few moments, and am now at your service if ready to start.

Jesse G. Jones
1842 -1917

"All right Reuben I will not encourage you but will warn you of the danger before us and inform you of the fact that we are up against the hard thing itsself. Let no noise betray us, follow me, when we reach the wall you must claw and pull for the top whilst I aid you with all my strength with a push. Our work must be done quickly, when over go to the left." Almost instantainously two men dropped outside, three or four guns fired, no harm was done except a few bruises from our sudden fall, all in a wad. "Follow me quickly don't you hear the Calvary bugle? they will search for us." Cumberland river was near us and a sand bar reached out half way across grew many weeds and brambly bushes affording a splendid hiding place. Whilst the calvery was making a mad rush to overtake the fleeing Jakeys we were completely submerged in water, slush, mud, weeds and brambles patiently awaiting our opportunity for travel. About three o'clock in the morning we decided they had given it up for the night after blocking every avenue of egress with pickets. We had now to avoid them by avoiding every road, path or opening, and shelter our movements in the dense foilage of the woods. Careful, causious and slow were our movements. What to do with ourselves when daylight dawned was a question to agitate and harasss our distracted minds. "Reuben we have almost reached our limit in this direction and must soon change ocourse. Our greatest danger is just besore us. I know that you are already fatigued and hungry and it would be an injustice to urge you on to a greater effort." "My comrade I am holding up remarkably well and am only too eager to obey your commands, what is it you would have us do?" "We must cross the Cumberland river at once if we aucceed in getting over we are safe for the present, if we stay here we are not." "Alright lead and I will follow, if we get drowned the difference in modes of death is too little to baffle over." We both could swim but were not experts in that line. By the friendly aid of a plank procured from a drift, we launched our craft for the other shore resolutely and determined. Daylight was too near on hand for any delay, we had to do our work briskly and secure a proper hiding for the day. We had traveled perhaps one mile from the river before halting. "Reuben excuse me, I forget that you are a sick man and need rest, we are about ready to take a whole day's rest for we must not attempt to travel today. We are yet in four miles of the Fort and hope that our enemies will be content with a fruitless search for us on the other side." I will not dwell on the torture and pangs hunger created, they were amelorated to a great degree by the good luck we had. Our thirst for liberty predominated every thing else and for it we could sacrifice all. "Hoping our success will continue for one more day, try to sleep a little Reuben it will strengthen you for tonight's work. I will be on guard to give the proper warning if exigencies require it." Thank God the sun was lowering in the western skies and our opportunity to renew our travel was near and wern't we glad that our persuers had not disturbed us. The exclusive woods route was the one for us we didn't want to make any mistake after so much success. We traveled slowly all night. In the early morning I said "Reuben you stay here while I go down to that house to get something to eat." I asked my friend at the house to excuse my early call for business was pressing and urgent I wanted a favor. Hunger had driven me to his house again, and a little food was badly needed whether it was cooked cold or raw mattered not and would alike be appreciated. "I am sorry that necefsity requires so much hast upon my part, for I have a great deal to tell you when I have the time and opportunity. There, there, you have plenty of food in that sack for which I thank you kindly, good bye." In a brisk walk I soon returned to Reuben and gave him a handfull of food and then let out at a lively gate for the thickets. "Reuben I feel happy and safe how do you feel?" "Oh! I feel happy too because I see you happy and think we both have grounds for rejoicing over our good luck." "It is true our job was no ordinary, one it was a credit to us to accomplish it so skillfully. A novis could not have done better. If Gen Oglesby did the evening of my arrest at the Fort call me a gump and gumpy this stigma has already preceeded me here and will be hard to down." When I was swimming the river it often echoed gump, gumpy. Take a view of the surrounding and see if nature ever produced more disireable place to hide in here we must eat, rest and sleep to recruit our jaded bodies. After which we can probe this thicket and acquaint ourselves with the strong holds for our defence. I will slip back to friend and see him. I did not have time when he issued the rashions. He is a worthy man and will do to trust through many of his neighbors are treacherous and must be avoided. You have lost so much sleep without nourishment, and fatigue without rest that quiet rest is what you need and must have and while I am off to see him do not worry with anxiety. Experience is a wonderful school and the lessons just learned is impressive and fruitfull for the better guidance of caution and vigilance. I will be gone two or three hours hoping to find you greatly refreshed on my return. "Friend is all quiet on the Patomic

Jesse G. Jones
1842 -1917

today? If so I will be relieved of a small part of my troubles. "So far as I know there is no cause for alarm through reports and rumer has it different, your troubles and escape with a comrade over at the Fort, is no known here and no doubt is greately exagerated. Yankees report they have you spotted and it is only a matter of time before they have you. It is also reported that you have had some recruits to your side. All sorts of prediction is rift nothing known deffinately. All is only speculation." "My friend you do me great favor by giving me any rumer for it is from them that I may make deductions, I seek no conflict with my enemy and would only by too glad to let him alone if he would let me. I will go south when the way is clear and if crowded I must neccessarly resist arrest through my chief aim is to act the good boy as far as circumstances will permit. Thanking you kindly for the interest you have manifested I must bid you good bye for the present and return to my comrade in the thickets." I found Reuben fast asleep snoaring at a frightful rate, shaking him remarked. "Good heavens Reuben wake up. I am glad to see you rest so well but with other men in the woods it is dangerous to snoar so loud. I expect Reuben that our friend learned a little news. It is quiet likely that we have some Confederates and some Yankee neighbors in this thicket. If I had any where else to go I would not mind it so bad. We have prior claim to them and a better right. We must try to see about it to morrow. If we should make entanglements with our Yankee Brothers before we get more amunition we would have only two shots each, half bluff and bullets, which works very well as long as it works at all, but is quiet risky. We had better now proceed to carefully inspect this Thicket, it stands us in hand to know all about it after we go through it to the east end and back here to the west end we will know whether it is a trap or a protection." We shouldered our guns military style and boldly walked with defiance. Our seclusion was too complete for our tremer of fear. "Reuben isn't this charming to be surrounded by the bresh briars, hazel nuts and grape vines and tangle weeds. I feel like I could whip a dozen yankees in here if I had plenty of amunition. We have had so much good luck I am certain that our Creator is on the Confederate side of the question. We were enjoying a happy dish of enthusiasm when sudently come the authoritative demand, "Hault surrender, or we will blow your brains out." Right before us stood six Yankee Soldiehs with guns presented demanding immediate unconditional surrender repugnant as the demand was we had no other alternative only to acquiest with heavy hearts and gloomy forebodings. We were striving to realize what had happened to us whilst the yankees were exulting over their victory and merrily rejoicing over their wonderful triumpth. "Boys are you good on double quick? eight or ten miles are before us and requires a test of our speed." "We are not experts in any drill manner but will do the best we can." One of the boys in blue acted as our pilot and the procession moved out in the direction of the Fort. The Yankee boys were mounted on good horses and we confederate chaps had to trudge our way through the entanglements of the thicket. The Yankees were hillarious and jovial, ready to laugh at any discomfiture befalling us. The excess of their merriment had proven the fore runner of disarter and thoughts of it acted as a tonic to our frustrated nerves. The pilot halted and warned his comrades that the surroundings wore a shroud of mystery and should be investigated before further progress. Three volunteers rode forward two remaind with us to see to our good behavior. A few moments later we heard some sharpo firing ahead of us. Our two Yankee gards looked mournfully sad when they saw only three out the four returning at full speed. The guards mounted their horses and left with them as their rear guard. Reuben and I was not long alone when two confederates dashed up with orders to remain. We were told by these men to remain where we were until friends could arrange matters to give us liberty and relief. Guns were distinctly heard in many directions. We were disarmed therefore unable to render help to our friends. After three hours patient waiting about ten confederates rode up to us addressing us in the following manner: "General Gumpy you have the liberty of this impregnable Fortress and are chosen as commander and chief of this division and we are ready to escort you to the General Headquarters. We owe a debt of gratitude to the boys who so gallently took us from the Yankee boys and think that they are in no dier need of a commander." "I am surprised to see so many comrades here in this isolated part of God's creation and am only too glad to unite wite them in the common defense of life and liberty I am opposed to wanten bloodshed and will skillfully avoid it when possible. Now tell me how many there are of your comrades we have." "About fifteen here and a reserved core of fifteen two miles from here." "If agreeable all round I think it is best to have a general meeting and have a thorough understanding with one another. We called for one

JESSE G. JONES
1842 -1917

volunteer to arrange the meeting. At nine in the morning at the reserve's headquarters." The meeting was called to order the following declarations of principles were adopted: "To mutually aid each other in the defense of personal liberty and to avoid aggressive warfare, and when the first opportunity presented itself with safety go across into Southern lines and we hereby refute the charge laid at our door of being bushwhackers and stigma was for prejudice, to fire the mind with odium and to render our cause more dispisable with everybody. The troopers now proceeded to elect two men for captains one for each squad of soldiers wits head quarters two miles apart. I was honored with one of the positions, and a man known as Restless Jack the other very few of these men knew one another and all had nick names. When we had any fighting on hand both camps were quickly consolidated. "Fellow comrades that which is of great improtance has not yet received much attention, Guns ammunition a few horses and a supply of food are all necessaries that we must have. We would like to hear from Restless Jack." "We have a surplus of all and can divide up with you boys. Our income may be depended on and will be requisite. We will now separate the camp and disband, "Reuben how are you standing the many ups and downs." "Very well, I guess, as I am stouter than when we started and feel much better" "I am indeed glad to hear it, and hope you will be at yourself in a few days preparation must commence at once to mount those without horses and equip those without guns we must be active in our work and thoroughly posted as to the movements of our enemies. I can find out a great deal of news over near the Fort by risking being caught. I am tempted to run the risk for the benefit to be derived. If no ill luck befalls me I will be gone about one day and two nights. The six Yankees who scooped down on us are not likely to renew their attack very soon, besides it does seem natural to think they would be content and let us alone as long as we behaved and disturbed nobody. Such however is not seriously expected and we must be prepared to meet any immergency. We must have a better souce of obtaining information than we now have and complete the many deatails incident to the battle field. I will have to make my trip on foot on account of the River to cross and recross. No Reuben I can do better alone and be safer in many ways. I want you boys to feel easy and be contented, this work must be done and I will do my best." That evening at twilight we were in a few steps of our friends house who had befriended us before. Our greetings congenial and sympathetic. As he had not seen nor heard of me he had supposed the fight in the thicket with the six Yankees had something to do in the change of affairs. In the briefest time possible I spun off to him a full account of the troubles of that day, in like manner he told all he knew about the Yankees movements he said they were determined to capture me and would put such a force in the field that no half dozen men could resist, he cautioned me to be on the lookout and asked me if there were favors wanted that night. I told him that I really needed a friend at the river as I was bound to cross it somewhere between ferries as the Yankees had control of them. He said that it might be possible for him to aid me in crossing about midnight. As he had a brother living on its bank who owned a private skiff and was a Confederate to the core. Under the shadows of night we found my friend's brother and was speedily set across and was promised a recrossing the next night at the same hour my prime motive for this trip was to make my final visit to see the Yankee Colonel before I undertook my chances through the Yankee lines and home gards on my way South. At the break of day I had gone through a diligent search for any evidence of any one else being there except the Col. and my conclusions were that the cost was clear. The good wife of the house was making her kitchen fire roar preparing her morning's meal when I appeared and kindly asked her if the Col. was at home and all others were absent. She replied he was, but yet in bed and no others were around as she knew. The Col hearing voices stormed out who is that and recieved the answer, "It is me," "Who is me?" "Y. Y. General Gumpy." I heard his feet strike the floor at once, "the biggest rascal and scoundrel that God ever let live present company you know is allways accepted Col" "What kind of news do you have now that you are here so early this morning." "I have a variety which is adapted to most any occasion. Your Judgment on them is what I seek and is why I am here so earley." As we sat at the table I remarked that I had in time passed eaten many good meals with them but some how I felt this was my last. I had plans formed and wanted the Col. to know them and receive this unbiased Judgement on them. I then bid the family goodbye and took the Col. out a short distance where in safety to us both we could talk. "My case Col. is gowing more serious every day, more difficult to maintain and requires a halt and change. I am made the pack horse for all crime and if I am caught must atone for other's sins. You

Jesse G. Jones
1842 -1917

have not doubt heard many exagerated accounts of me and many pure down falsehoods too." "Yes, I often hear of you but never hear anything good, it is always bitter and bad for the cause I am in and under such circumstances I don't see how I am to render you any aid without violating my pledge of loyalty in the army." "The position you take certainly debars me from pressing any other questions. We still retain our great friendship for one another. Col. I give you my hand in good by, I must be going." We separated going opposite directions. The balance of the day we spent on the river waiting for our friend to come after night and put us across. He was punctual and we had not long to wait. We pressed forward to where the boys were camped while it was dark and arrived there before day light. Reuben met me first and seemed overwhelmed with joy to see me safely returned. He was full of news, ten new recruits and had been added to our ranks. Reckless Jack had had a fight a fight and had brought in ten or twelve head of horses but strange to say no prisoners. All arrangements were now made to arm, mount, and equip every one of us. Reckless Jack had sent word to me that he would be over and exchange reports that morning, both wings of the camp were to be together for a brief time. Reckless Jack remarked to me he and the boys had come to pay me a visit but had doubted very much of finding me at home. "Those fellows over there ought to know by now that they can't keep you when they get you and it is useless to waste time on you." "I thank you boys for coming for I want to impart some knowledge which if heeded may be alike profitable to all. We have so far been victorious in all of our little engagements with the yankees, the cause for it is appparent when we consider how far in the dark they are as to our strength. Their courage is to be commended but what about their judgement. They talk it loud that to make a quick clean wipe out extermination twenty-five men should try us. There are a few citizen spies around us who report to the Fort that we are very few in number, not more than five or six. We would like to hear Reckless Jack's report of yesterday's fight and causalities. He replied that there was more running than fighting, and there were 12 Yankees and 20 Confederates engaged resulting in the capture of 12 horses and 12 stand of arms. The Yankees were relieved of their guns and horses and ordered back to the Fort where they could rig up and try us again. "You acted wisely and prudent for no other course was opened to you. We had better have out some scouts for fear of a surprise. The east and west end of the thicket should be well scouted every day. When we are not engaged in defending ourselves we ought to learn all the strong holds so we can appropriate them to our uses when necessary; also we have friends and enemies among the citizens and they should be know individualy and readily discaiminated from each other. Reuben if you and one more will accompany me to the west end where you and I made our first camp we can do all necessary scouting and leave the east end to be cared for by Reckless Jack." We saw no visible marks of the enemy and kept a diligent watch all along our route to the old camp. "Here boys you must stop for one half hour while I go and see my old friend one mile away, keep your vigilence." In less that a half hour the boys saw me coming in haste. "Mount your horses boys and follow me." We dashed up to where all the boys were loitering around taking the world easy. "I want 25 volenteers quick saddle up and with a full supply of ammunition follow me to the east end of the thicket." A few guns were heard in that direction. On we sped with all the haste the rough ground and tangle thicket would permit closer and closer we grew to a minature battle field where the contestants were about equally matched all around in grit and determination as well as in numbers. Every avenue of escape was cut off and a fight to the finish was the only way out. They consolidated their forces and plunged at us with all the frenzy of mad men and were resisted by equal courage and desperation of the confederates. Nothing had been seen of Reckless Jack and scouts, his horse had been seen with other dead horses. The battle ceased and a search was made for the Captain. He was found in a pocket or cave in a very rough part of the mountain. He stated that he had lost one of his noble boys and his favorite horse just as we came to his assistance. He wanted to know how many of the boys had lost their lives and how many Yankees had escaped to their stronghold. On being informed that none got away and three of our brave boys were killed and the Yankee loss was about half of their number and a full half of their horses. We returned to our camps full of sorrow over our losses. Reckless Jack could not understand how we could know of his troubles and come to his rescue so quickly. I informed him of the fact that I had friends whose delight was to keep me posted on all their movements. The Yankees are learning every day more and more about our strength and we may expect larger forces to fight each succeeding battle. Their means for recruits is unlimited, ours is quite limited it would be suicide to continue our course here against such odds. We must do more thinking and less fighting. I am expecting a change in their tactics. they have discussed

Jesse G. Jones
1842 -1917

among themselves the plausability of attacting us at the break of day, and to have 40 or 50 volunteers to do the job. Every soldier here must feel himself called upon to be in fighting trim at a moment's call while I am looking out for news of warning and will be prompt to report and take charge of half the men. Keep up your courage and vigilence, for it is the main stay in a soldiers life. Capt Reckless Jack aided the boys in preparing for another hard engagement for I felt like it was coming and nothing is so beneficial as to be ready. Our boys will number about 40, enough to make an interesting battle with 50 Yankee boys for we know the thicket. "My case Col. is gowing more serious every day, more difficult to maintain and requires a halt and change. I am made the pack horse for all crime and if I am caught must atone for other's sins. You have not doubt heard many exagerated accounts of me and many pure down falsehoods too." "Yes, I often hear of you but never hear anything good, it is always bitter and bad for the cause I am in and under such circumstances I don't see how I am to render you any aid without violating my pledge of loyalty in the army." "The position you take certainly debars me from pressing any other questions. We still retain our great friendship for one another. Col. I give you my hand in good by, I must be going." We separated going opposite directions. The balance of the day we spent on the river waiting for our friend to come after night and put us across. He was punctual and we had not long to wait. We pressed forward to where the boys were camped while it was dark and arrived there before day light. Reuben met me first and seemed overwhelmed with joy to see me safely returned. He was full of news, ten new recruits and had been added to our ranks. Reckless Jack had had a fight a fight and had brought in ten or twelve head of horses but strange to say no prisoners. All arrangements were now made to arm, mount, and equip every one of us. Reckless Jack had sent word to me that he would be over and exchange reports that morning, both wings of the camp were to be together for a brief time. Reckless Jack remarked to me he and the boys had come to pay me a visit but had doubted very much of finding me at home. "Those fellows over there ought to know by now that they can't keep you when they get you and it is useless to waste time on you." "I thank you boys for coming for I want to impart some knowledge which if heeded may be alike profitable to all. We have so far been victorious in all of our little engagements with the yankees, the cause for it is apprarent when we consider how far in the dark they are as to our strength. Their courage is to be commended but what about their judgement. They talk it loud that to make a quick clean wipe out extermination twenty-five men should try us. There are a few citizen spies around us who report to the Fort that we are very few in number, not more than five or six. We would like to hear Reckless Jack's report of yesterday's fight and causalities. He replied that there was more running than fighting, and there were 12 Yankees and 20 Confederates engaged resulting in the capture of 12 horses and 12 stand of arms. The Yankees were relieved of their guns and horses and ordered back to the Fort where they could rig up and try us again. "You acted wisely and prudent for no other course was opened to you. We had better have out some scouts for fear of a surprise. The east and west end of the thicket should be well scouted every day. When we are not engaged in defending ourselves we ought to learn all the strong holds so we can appropriate them to our uses when necessary; also we have friends and enemies among the citizens and they should be know individualy and readily discaiminated from each other. Reuben if you and one more will accompany me to the west end where you and I made our first camp we can do all necessary scouting and leave the east end to be cared for by Reckless Jack." We saw no visible marks of the enemy and kept a diligent watch all along our route to the old camp. "Here boys you must stop for one half hour while I go and see my old friend one mile away, keep your vigilence." In less that a half hour the boys saw me coming in haste. "Mount your horses boys and follow me." We dashed up to where all the boys were loitering around taking the world easy. "I want 25 volenteers quick saddle up and with a full supply of ammunition follow me to the east end of the thicket." A few guns were heard in that direction. On we sped with all the haste the rough ground and tangle thicket would permit closer and closer we grew to a minature battle field where the contestants were about equally matched all around in grit and determination as well as in numbers. Every avenue of escape was cut off and a fight to the finish was the only way out. They consolidated their forces and plunged at us with all the frenzy of mad men and were resisted by equal courage and desperation of the confederates. Nothing had been seen of Reckless Jack and scouts, his horse had been seen with other dead horses. The

Jesse G. Jones
1842 -1917

battle ceased and a search was made for the Captain. He was found in a pocket or cave in a very rough part of the mountain. He stated that he had lost one of his noble boys and his favorite horse just as we came to his assistance. He wanted to know how many of the boys had lost their lives and how many Yankees had escaped to their stronghold. On being informed that none got away and three of our brave boys were killed and the Yankee loss was about half of their number and a full half of their horses. We returned to our camps full of sorrow over our losses. Reckless Jack could not understand how we could know of his troubles and come to his rescue so quickly. I informed him of the fact that I had friends whose delight was to keep me posted on all their movements. The Yankees are learning every day more and more about our strength and we may expect larger forces to fight each succeeding battle. Their means for recruits is unlimited, ours is quite limited it would be suicide to continue our course here against such odds. We must do more thinking and less fighting. I am expecting a change in their tactics. they have discussed among themselves the plausability of attacting us at the break of day, and to have 40 or 50 volunteers to do the job. Every soldier here must feel himself called upon to be in fighting trim at a moment's call while I am looking out for news of warning and will be prompt to report and take charge of half the men. Keep up your courage and vigilence, for it is the main stay in a soldiers life. Capt Reckless Jack aided the boys in preparing for another hard engagement for I felt like it was coming and nothing is so beneficial as to be ready. Our boys will number about 40, enough to make an interesting battle with 50 Yankee boys for we know the thicket. Three minutes later pandamonium reigned in that house and the situation was beyond immediate comprehention not much less was the condition in woods my only advantage was I knew every inch of the woods. I knew that I would be pursued and my first consideration was to secure arms for defense, I knew where some had been stored before and if still there would supply my wants. With all haste I went and secured what I wanted comprising of two double barrel shot guns and two six shooters with plenty of ammunition. Some of the confederate boys were still in hiding places and the woods were being scouted for all. Very frequently the searchers werer in 40 or 50 yards of me and did not see me. I did not attempt to travel but to depend on dodging and hiding. The thorns, briars and many other kind of tormenters tore my clothes into threads. I also lost my hat and socks and had to walk on the tops of my boots while the saw briars shreaded the hide on my ankles. I neither had a needle, pin, pocket knife, pocket book nor a cent of money in this plight. I slept in a cornfield about 200 yards from where I made my break. I knew it would not do to try to travel at night all the ways out would be watched. At day break the second day I was one mile from where I started where I proposed to lie close and await developments and possed the day in mending my clothes by skining the bark of young hickories with my fingers and using locus thorns for needles, my success was astonishing from a servicable standpoint. From an artistic stand point reprehensible and disgusting. I lived on blackberries and green apples, the berries too ripe and the apples too green. I saw the soldiers hunting me and heard one of them inquire of another man as far from him as I was if I had been heard from or seen. The third morning I was a mile further and spent another day in hunger and seclusion. The fourth morning found me four miles off. The country now before me was very open and dangerous according to my tactics. The timber had been taken for the iron works with the exception of about 100 acres in the middle that was yet dense thicket. I was trying to go a due north course and the thickets was on my way, how to get to it without taking too much risk was what bothered me. After carefully surveying the surroundings made an effort to go when in fifty yards of it looked back and was houror stricken to see about 50 yankees on my persuit. Low and high places prevented them from seeing me enter the thicket. Instead of going in I droped down at the edge under alder bushes, weeds and briars, my greatest fear was their horses tramping on me. As I had supposed they circled the thicket one of them sat on his horse in ten feet of me but was in a short time moved further on. I had discovered in coming a gully that run pararallel to the rout I come, the mouth of which was close to me. I begun to crawfise and kept at it until I was certain that I could make better speed otherwise. After keeping the gully for a half hour I left it and went down on Cumberland river and decided to cross it. I found a slab in a drift and with hickory bark fastened my guns and amunition on it and proceeded to cross. Things were not as I had supposed, and I readily realized my mistake and decided at once to return to the other shore the same old puncheon was again called on to do service and I was soon across but had the misfortune to have my guns

Jesse G. Jones
1842 -1917

and amunition soaked with water. I droped the hole outfit in the river and went down the river trying to keep a northern course I rested that night some 8 or 10 miles from where I started, bright hopes were dawning. Bright hopes and prospects sweet are seen, In distant fields all rich and lovely; But adverse waves rolls between, That thwarts my voyage stormy, Contested hopes must I submit To the iron grasp of dispair. Say, oh say, must I contently sit And not a solum vow declare? No not I, whilst I live I will command, Ambition, energy and frithfully persvere Till I extricate myself and span Across the furoious waves that interfere. The above lines were the result of my thoughts after a close inspection of my suit of clothes. The bark threads had dried, twisted and kinked out of all shape and no one would have been able to judge the style I wore. It was necessary now for me to avoid all, whether friend or foe until I reached the place of destination, which was 35 or 40 miles ahead of me. If I reached that place I was sure of meeting a friend worthy of the name. I could make better time from that on through a little river 25 or 30 yards wide was to cross very often. Without hesitation I swam it and kept a straight direction north. At dark I discovered a big plain road runing exctly the direction I wanted to go. After resting a while and waiting for belated travelers to quit the road and yurn inyo their homes. I thought I would risk the road as it was so much smoother traveling. I passed two or three farm houses unobserved and done my first foraging at one of their milk houses which was well stocked with good goods. I traveled on 3 or 4 miles unobserved and unmolested and discovered my road was leading me down into a dense bottom working alive with mesquitos. I wanted day light but could not afford to wait for it among those blood suckers. I finally came to a little river which was from 30 to 40 yards wide as I did not see any ferryboat supposed it was a ford. As the night was dark I could not see across to know anythang about the getting out place. I had not long to tarry or to decide the question. I got a small pole and used as a walking stick keeping it before me in order to know when I could wade and when I had to swim. To my great surprize I found no place over 12 inches deep on this side there were no swampy bottom and after going a mile or two from the river was away from the mesquitos. I was now15 or 16 miles from where I started all o.k. so far. My first attention now was to do more reparing to my suit. Just before day that morning I passed through the out skirts of Hopkinsville, Ky., and from there on had move or less knowledge of the country which meant a great deal to a man travelidg by guess. I kept a bee line through the woods and the large plantations and as I would see objects once familiar the move brisk was my gait. Two years before I had lived where I was pulling for and a chum mate was still there who would receive me with open arms. The seventh evening was passing and I skipped along rejoicing I was now in 14 miles of my objective point and thought one more day would wind up a race for life and liberty. The bitter hardships I had undergone were all obscured by the prospects of better days. Tom Easly my friend was not aware of my coming and the night of the eighth was suprised at midnight by hearing some one hollowing hello! hello! at the gate. "Hey, hey, come in" "Is that you Tom." "Yes" he said, "well come out here first, I want to speak to you privately and then go in. "Is there any Yankees on the premises."? "no," he said and in his friendly way was holding my hand and said my voice familiar and when he got me to the light he would know me. "No Tom you wan't for you will be carred away with my haughty apparel and cosy suit. We hurried on in to Tom's room where he lost no time in lighting the lamp, he with looks of astonishment and consternation threw his arms around my neck exlaiming "my old chum, oh how stupid in me not to have guessed you when I was told all about the times you have been having, no longer than yesterday. "Who was it Tom that had so much knowledge?" He gave me the name of Charles Childers. He said you had gone South. Without another word Tom turned and opened his trunk, drew from it a costly cloth suit for Sunday wear. "There"said he, "we used to wear one anothers clothes as we are the same size. Put these on." "I will exchange suits with you Tom but it is mortifying to me to swindle as good a friend. You must excuse the lack of a hat suspenders and socks to my wardrobe." Tom was carefully; arranging my discarded suit to go in his trunk. "What on earth are you trying to do Tom, the stiff bark takes up room and I find the trunk full small. Why do you want them in there?" "To take special care of them for they are far more valuable to me than the one I gave you, they tell a tale of love and friendship they remind us of those perlious times and shows us truly neccessity to be the mother of invention." I looked in the mirror and did not know myself. I was neither hungry nor sleepy. We talked until day. Tom owned about 100 slaves and they would know me. We planed to go to his brothers for breakfast four miles off. We went to the barn to catch our horses. Tom saddled up

Jesse G. Jones
1842 -1917

his best horse and told me to mount him as a present. We let out at a lively gait, met his brother John, he had quising to do to get at the true status of things. Tom said he must go to a near by town and get some money for me. John said he had money and would cheerfully devide. Tom objected to any one contributing a cent as he wanted to have the pleasure all to himself. Three hours afterwards Tom returned with a cart load of dry goods to deck me out and had a roll of greenback as big as my arm. "Tom you must take this clothing back about one extra shirt is all that I can be encumbered with. As to the money only a few dollars is all sufficient for I am likely to be captured at any time." He handed me a little roll but beged me to accept more. On a closer examination I discovered the roll had $185.00 some were large bills. I told him the amount was too much and for him to take some of it back he positively refused to do so and said he would rather double the amount. I learned that this country was equally divided on the war question but Yankees were riding around over it making very little distuubance. I thought it best for me not to stop for fear some one might recognize me and breed trouble to my friends as well as to myself. I kept close to avoid any one seeing me. We arranged to go north about 35 miles where Tom's sister lived. As I was never known there except by the family. I stood a better chance to rest up and become once more normal in my appetite and sleep. For many days and nights they affectionately watched over me, often pulling me away from the table, and rousing me from unatural slumber . I put salve on my ankles and legs to heal up the scratches inflicted by the saw briars. After two weeks rest I wanted to try my skill in worming my way south. Tom and I would reason the matter over and over without coming to any tenable conclusion. Tom would beg me to give the undertaking up and stay with him until a better showing presented itself. He did not know that loving friends were morning me as dead, day after day we would scan the west, the south and the east for a weak gap to go through. "Tom I must start in the morning and trust to luck I'll try some way if it be north." Tom would not listen to me leaving the horse and to gratify him I agreed to ride to the Cumberland River and if I could cross with him without a pass then go on. I knew I could not and so prepared myself for it by taking a young man with me to report back to Tom. In tears Tom and our friends parted on arriving at the ferry, I was told promptly a pass was demanded. We dropped down the river 3 or 4 miles from the ferry where I discharged the young man and requested of him to take Tom's horse back to him for if I kept him I surely would be taken. With a message of thanks from me to Tom he and I parted. I was put across the river in a canoe by a citizen 12 or 15 miles above the mouth. The Tennessee river runs parallel with the Cumberland both empting into the Ohio 12 miles apart. Between the two rivers all low bottom land no improvements while I was taking a short rest in a little thicket mooding over transpiring events discovered a man in a few feet of me apparently doing the same thing. It is said misery loves compay and our greetings surely supported that idea. After a few words we both learned that we wanted to cross the Ohio river and had the same place selected to make our crossing. A negro influenced by a little silver money put us across from the Kentucky to Illinois banks. We grew chumy but made slow progress toward knowledge of each other's business. By slow degrees we picked up dots here and there that gave a clue and a basis for supposition. Illinois was having an upheavel in home affairs. The Copper-heads were making the trouble. They refused to go to the Federal army and help coerse the southern states back into the union. They were strong state-right people. Valandingham was at the head of the party and he was very strong. My partner in trouble thought I was either a Copperhead or a Confederate. He expressed himself as being an uncompromising Copper-head himself and had been run out of Indiana two weeks before for being so and had been down in Kentucky trying the virtues of the state's neutrality. He insisted on us remaining togather as long as our sentiments did not cross. I told him that I could tolerate anything except Federalism and I was willing to continue the journal with him to Indiana and study conditions existing with the people. He reminded me to keep a still tongue and a wise head for we were approaching a veritable volcano. I assured him that I was not altogather without practical knowledge down that line and would try to prove worthy of all confidence reposed in me. A bad state of affairs disturbed the country. Life was in danger, people hiding out in the woods and I was forceably reminded of former days. After a long consultation with my Copper-head brother I decided to go north and keep going until I found a more tranquil element. This friend insisted on my taking letters of introduction to his brother in Ohio. With a kind farewell from Indiana in due time reached Ohio and found the brother as expected a full-fledged Copper-head. By this time I had gotton enough

Jesse G. Jones
1842 -1917

stock in other people's business and was willing to change tactics a little. I confessed at once that I was a Confederate soldier and wanted to return south. The Copper-heads were willing to render me any help but stood no better chance than I did myself, for I stood higher in the Federal soldier's estimation that they did. After three of four days of hard study and reflections over the matter decided to run the risk of going back to Dixie Land. Mapping out a route, went off the Tenessee river exposed to Federal troop home guards for more than 300 miles, I cannot say that I was not scared all the time and felt as skittish as a wild buck for through a large portion of the country I was well known. I crossed the Ohio river a few miles above the mouth of the Tennessee river and ten miles up the Tennessee crossed to the west side of it. In settling the ferry bill it was necessary to go to a little grocery store to make change, here I saw about twenty men merry and lively, they eyed me closely I done them the same way. They were evidently afraid of me and I know I was afraid of them for I took them to be Yankees and they took me to be a Yankee. If I had been 100 yards away I could have done some runing. They were northern men trying to get south to join the southern army. I was trying to do the same thing but wanted more caution and less whiskey in mine as the Yankees were thick all over that portion of Kentucky. Keeping them in the dark I evaded their company and at Como, Tenn., heard the great Metherd, a former U. S. Senator. He was a gifted orator and a rabid Unionist. He flayed the South for what was out and belittled the sesession move. He scored the Confederate soldeirs, his audience being chiefly Yankee soldiers who was carried away with his eloquence and lustily cheered him. For policy sake I joined in with them the only instance during the war that such charge could have been laid at my door. Being a little refreshed by the eloquence of my enemy continued my journey south, often meeting Yankees I was well stocked with all kinds of stories suited to different occasions and was fairly posted on war times generally. A man waith a six-mule team drove out of a field into the road before me. He was loaded with ear corn and kindly asked me if I wanted ride and thinking he belonged in the neighborhood I accepted his kind offer. I found him to a sedate kind of a fellow that would talk only when questioned. Having graveled one mile or more I said to him, "How far down this road do you go?" "About 50 miles," he replied. "Do you go the Clifton road?" I asked. "Yes I am going there." I told him I had a sick brother there and was trying to get to him, without being asked a question I told him that my brother belonged to the 2nd Ky. regiment. A small squad of Yanke soldiers met us in the road, they did not bother us but listened attentively to one of my best spun stories. We camped out and I helped with the team. What worried me most was my friend had not a word to say to me or anyone else while it was my aim to impress everybody that I was a Yankee or a sympathiser. Wee were crossing the Tennesse river over into Clifton. He turned to me and asked if I was acqainted in Clifton. "No," I answered. "Well permit me to introduce one of my best friends to you." I thanked him and said I would be glad to form the acquaintance of any of his friends. He looked around and called out. "Come here Dock," and he approached us and I received the introduction. He was all business and as quick as double trigers as he whist off said for me to follow him, which I did in a turkey trot. He kept up his brisk gait and landed in a big store which was doing a big business, making no halt in the front part but kept on to the counting room, told me to take a seat and in the same haste snatched up a pen and done some writing. In the short space of ten minutes he was out and ready and said for me to come with him. After going 200 yards on pavement we turned to one side and entered a beautiful yard that contained one of the most costly dwellings of the town. Into the house we bolted and without much ceremony dropped in our seats at the dinner table. He ate like he walked and our meal was soon over. Into a private room of the house we went, he turned and asked what he could do for me. I replied that I wanted to get through the Yankee lines into north Alabama. He said thae the country was chuckful of Yankees and home guard and for me to follow him upstairs where I could have a private room? He said to me "I want you to keep close in this room, don't come down about the store or out side of this yard, and patiently wait until I find an opportunity to go. This is critical work and must be managed exactly right or it will result bad to both of us. It may be one day and again one or two weeks." He dashed off down to the store and left me alone in my room with an abundant supply of books and papers. I comprehended the situation exactly and determined not to worry the Doctor with any questions. He came regular to his meals, always had a cheerful greeting for me but not a word otherewise. Two weeks had passed when he ate his dinner as usual and went back to the store, in ten or fifteen minutes he returned in great haste, "Your opportunity is at hand. In less that ten minutes a two-horse wagon will pass the gate, the horse next to the house is a baldfaced sorrel the other a dark brown, be ready when it

Jesse G. Jones
1842 -1917

comes, you must not speak to the man or stop him to get on, crawl up on the spring seat by the side of him. "Here Doctor Childers I want to pay you." "I don't want to hear any more of that, do as I tell you." And away he went to the store. The Doctor's good wife bade me good bye and with her I left a message of thanks for the Doctor. The wagon arrived I climbed upon the spring seat, the man who was driving did not even look toward me but kept his eyes straight forward. The Bugle and the drum with other army rackets nor the crowded street had any effect on our adamantine look. We werer about to cross a picket line when the guard stormed out the familiar words, "Halt, have you passes gentelmen?" I felt a tremor shake me from circumference to center for I was totally in the dark. My associate, in an unconcerned manner fumbled in his pockets and produced a strip of paper and handed it to the guard after careful examination the guard passed it back to him and said pass on gentlemen. We passed two other picket lines in the same manner and with the same results still we had not looked at each other or spoke a word. After we had traveled 4 or 5 miles and was through all picket lines we met a scouting party they too called for our passes, after a careful examination they gave them back with the old familiar words, pass on gentlemen. We were then where it supposed we would not be bothered in showing passes. I was much relieved of anxiety if I was in the dark. So far everything had gone favorable and what need had I to know more. My partner turned and looked at me and laughed. "Oh! Reuben, Reuben how I am surprised a this strange meeting. Four weeks ago 100 miles North of here we parted company, with little or no expectation of ever seeing one another again, and here are still sailing around on Terra Firma with our life preservers on amidst our enemies and with authority to go where we please. I do not comprehend how you have managed to be so clever, it seems that you have blended business with escape." "I have had to resort to all sorts of intrigue for safety," said Reuben, "remember my instructor was an expert to whom I am indebted for success." "What about the wagon and team?" "They were community property at our old homestead or head-quarters." "Have you been back there Reuben?" "Certainly, to know whether you did escape or not, fragments of the disbanded crew were quickly consolidated by Reckless Jack for your release and those Yankee guards will never know how near death's door they stood. The news of your successful escape spread from friend to friend as well as from foe to foe, the former rejoiceing in exultation, the other dismayed with chagrin over results. With much haste I withdrew from this frenzied mob, with the outfit you see, to beat my way South peddling on chickens eggs and butter, visiting all at the Yankee camps, who seemed to sympathize with me as I was a cripple in my legs and walked with a crutch." "I see Reuben traffic was good, for you have even traded your old red head for a black one. Ah! indeed Reuben I see there are more ways to kill a cat than by choking it to death on butter. I am so thankful that our hardships have not been altogather in vain, we have much to regret but more to be thankful for. This four month's effort to free ourselves from Fort Donalson is about accomplished; the end is almost in sight." We were on the South line of Tennessee and Alabama and Mississippi is just before us. Our friends and loved ones there stood ready with open arms to greet us. Fifteen miles West of Laurenceburgh Tennesse was the most painful ordeal of all, we had to part, Reuben going to North Miss. and I to North Ala. Let the curtain drop, my last view of Reuben Tucker of Guntown Miss. was a thing of the past. I stood erect and as rigid as an Egyptian statue, confused and unable to see my way clear for a few minutes. I knew that both armies scouted the country intervening between me and Rogersvill Ala. my nearest haven of refuge. I also knew that I was more likely than not to meet up with the dreaded Yankees. After weighing the matter carefully I decided to venture and trust to Gumpy luck. With a spontaneous flow of new courage I entered the home stretch race determined and resolute to win or lose all. I gained the victory and thereby avoided 18 months prisoner life at Camp Douglas Chicago. After three or four days rest I reentered the Confederate service with the 7th Ala. Cavalry. I received a bad wound at Murfesboro but was not discharged till the 15th of May 1865 at Donville Ala. The war closed the country wassss ruined and devastation met the gaze of starved naked and pennyless soldiers. I sought out new fields in Tex. where the armies had not made its blight and others in like manner helped swell the tremendous influx to Texas. People rushing here from every quarter of the globe subjected one to incidents strange and peculiar you would never know who you was talking before. Fifteen years after the war I met that prince of good fellows, Dr. Aca Childers, who so kindly befriended me at

Jesse G. Jones
1842 -1917

Clifton Tenn. He kept me hid in his house for two weeks though the town and country was full of Yankees, he was a leading business man and redily got the good will and confidence of either friend or foe. I received papers from him which carried me safely through the Yankee lines anywhere. Again, there is another incident I wish to make known to my readers, 25 years after the war while I was traveling around over Texas in a two horse wagon one evening chanced to stop and camp a little early, convience being unusually good, it was a lonely place, no house in sight, wood and water were plentiful. I had just started my fire when a man in a two horse wagon drove up and said that I had an execellent place to camp, and he would like to camp with me if I had no objections. "All right sir I am thankful to have your company." We soon adjusted matters and arranged our supper together, and in the most chummy manner engaged in laughing and talking as well as eating. When bedtime came he asked if I thought it would rain, adding he was subject to rheumatism and had to avoid getting wet, and had no wagon sheet. "Very well you may bunk with me if you don't mind being a little crowded." "Many thanks for your proposition as I see you have a good sheet." We were soon wedged together in my wagon, he said that he was not sleepy a bit, and the way his tongue rattled off incidents of daring was convincing. So much gass soon got old with me, and his most wonderful deeds ceased to provoke more than a groan or a yawn, he said, "look here partner I see you have a stiff arm, what caused it?" "A Yankee bullet at Murfresboro." "Where did you get crippled so in your hips?" "Near Fort Donalson, by a bushwhacker. You bet I fixed him." "And did you kill him?" "I did, and I'm proud of it." "And arn't you afraid of haunts?" "No. There is no such thing." "In the name of all that is good that bushwhacker spirit is hovering around you to-night; it was the self-same spirit you fired on at the corner of the house and the self-same spirit to protect the dying soldier." Recognition was instenataneous with us both and I would have been first to split the wind had I lost my opportunity for an even star-. Here I will drop the pen.

John F. Kane
1838 - 1902

At Chambersburg, Pennsylvania on October 17, 1863 John Kane signed a substitute volunteer enlistment for Jesse S. Baer agreeing to serve in Baer's place for a "sufficient consideration." His enlistment in the 148th Pennsylvania Volunteer Infantry, Company D, is dated November 13, 1863. John's military records indicate he deserted on April 28, 1864, however, he must have returned to his unit since he was officially discharged on June 11, 1865 at Harrisburg.

At the time of John Kane's enlistment the regiment was transferred from the First to the Third Brigade and two different detachments of conscripts, numbering about 280, were added bringing it up to it's original strength. The regiment participated in several minor battles and went into winter quarters at Stevensburg. In the spring of 1864 they received more recruits. The time was spent in drill and parade until the evening of the 3d of May when they moved from camp. The next day they acted as skirmishers and reached the battlefield of the Wilderness. The following day they acted as support to the other troops. On the 9th they arrived on the Spotsylvania Road at the Poe River. Here the regiment was ordered to take the heights on the other side of the river. They forded it under great difficulties, and notwithstanding the heavy fire received from the Rebel battery they advanced steadily, putting the enemy to route. Late in the day the battle was renewed, the enemy coming out of the woods opposite, and were met with a withering volley by Captain George A Bayard's Company. The whole regiment opened fire. The enemy, moving into some works, returned the fire with deadly effect. Nightfall put a stop to this fiercely contested though unimportant battle, the loss being 200 men. On the 12th a grand assault was made on the enemy's works. In this attack Lieutenant Colonel Fairlamb was wounded while pressing forward in front of his men. The remainder of the month they were engaged in marching and fighting, sustaining some loss, and on the 3d of June they arrived in front of Cold Harbor and by a brilliant charge they captured the front line of the enemy, but it being amply provided with every facility for defense they were obliged to fall back. Here, owing to the loss of a commander, Colonel Beaver was promoted to the command of the Third Brigade but was shortly after wounded. Soon after this the Second Corps joined in movement upon the Jerusalem Plank Road and took a position, erecting a line of fortifications, but the enemy being alert for an advantage, saw a brake, struck bravely, causing much disorder, which resulted in the capture or Colonel Frazer and Captain George A. Bayard. On the 28th of July, the Second Corps attacked the enemy across the James in which several guns were taken. A few days after the Corps again crossed the river attacking the enemy at Strawberry Plains but they soon returned and were pushed out onto the Weldon Railroad, from there they were hastily taken to Ream's Station. Immediately upon their arrival the enemy emerged from the woods in front in excellent order but was repulsed. The Regiment was then assigned the duty of skirmishers to ascertain the enemy's position. They soon found that the enemy had formed two lines of battle preparing for an attack. In a short time a deadly fire was begun along the whole line and the enemy was forced to retreat but they soon returned in double column, in a closed mass, with an unwavering front; volleys of lead were hurled at their ranks but despite their terrible loss they continued to advance until they reached the outer edge of the works. Here a hand, to hand conflict ensued, though manfully defended the division fell back. It was in this desperate struggle that Colonel Beaver, who had just returned and resumed command was severely wounded, losing a leg. Soon after General Hancock, who being familiar with the efficient service rendered by the 148th Regiment, directed that

John F. Kane
1838 - 1902

they should be armed with Spencer repeating rifles. On the 27th of October a detachment from this Regiment, under Captain J. Z. Brown, was selected to assault the enemy's line in the front. Having arranged his men for the desperate attack, he dashed forward, drove back the opposing pickets, scaled the ramparts, capturing four commissioned officers, and more men than he had led to the encounter. The enemy receiving aid from the other forts forced them to retire. Upon the opening of the Spring 1865 campaign they moved to Hatchers Run and latter to the Adam's Farm. On the 2nd of April they passed through the enemy's line and reached Southern Station where they found the enemy determined to make a stand. Here the Second Brigade again led. They were met with a terrific fire, checking its advance, killing and wounding large numbers. This disaster induced General Miles, to detach the 148th. He ordered it to advance, Captain Sutton having command of the right wing, and Captain Harper of the left. They moved courageously forward and by a strategically maneuver, flanked the enemy's works, and with a withering fire from the repeating rifles, caused the entire brigade to throw down its arms and surrender. On the following day, General Miles publicly commended the gallant conduct of the 148th, also announcing the result of the charge to be 700 prisoners, pieces of artillery and two flags. After this it was ordered to do detail work and afterwards took part in the battle of Farmersville and other miner engagements of the campaign, until the 3rd of June, not until after the surrender of Lee, was it mustered out, near Alexandria.

John Kane died in 1902.

John Morgan Kefover
1843 - 1877

John Morgan Kefover was born in Woodside, Fayette County, Pennsylvania on June 18, 1843, to Thomas and Sarah Harrison Kefover. He was the eldest son and with his father worked the family farm. Their farm was in close proximity to the farm where his Great-Grandfather Jacob (Kefauver) Kefover settled in the 1780s from Frederick, Maryland. Morgan was the second in the family of six - Isabelle, Anna, Ophelia, and his brothers Pierce and Plummer. One week after his eighteenth birthday he enlisted, on June 24, 1861, in Uniontown, Fayette County, Pennsylvania, as a private in Company G, 11th Regiment, Pennsylvania Reserve Corps.

After a year of service with the Union Army Morgan was captured at Gaines Mill, Virginia, spending his nineteenth birthday confined at Richmond, Virginia. After two months in Richmond he was paroled at Aikens Landing, Virginia on August 5, 1862. In less than two weeks he was back with his Regiment and was wounded at Bull Run, Virginia. Shot in his right hand tearing away his middle finger. Morgan was treated at a Convalescent Camp in Alexandria, Virginia and was hospitalized for 61 days. On November 13, 1862, Morgan was discharged from the Union Army due to his disability in Alexandria, Virginia. Returning to his family in Pennsylvania he continued to work with his father on their farm for a little over a year. Becoming discontented he followed his Uncle James Kefover to Muscatine, Iowa, a place where many of his aunts, uncles, and cousins would also settle.

JOHN MORGAN KEFOVER
1843 - 1877

Shortly after his moving to Iowa he re-enlisted as a private with the 6th Iowa Calvary, Company B. Since his previous battle injury prevented him from handling a saber or a rifle, he worked in the "Chow Hall." He served in the Dakota Territories and was discharged on October 17, 1865 in Sioux City, Iowa.

John Morgan Kefover married Laura Melissa Steffy on August 28, 1866 in Wilton Junction, Muscatine County, Iowa. To the couple five children were born: Anna, Allie, Plummer, Myrtle, and John Morgan Jr. Morgan applied for and received a pension on November 9, 1869, receiving $3.00 a month. He died at age 34 of consumption on November 17, 1877, two days before his son John Morgan Jr. was born.

NATHANIEL KING
1838 - 1923

Nathaniel King was born May 23, 1838 in Somerset County, Pennsylvania, the son of David and Eliza Graft King. On August 30, 1862 he enlisted in Company B, 77th Pennsylvania Volunteer Infantry (Sharpshooters) and is said to have walked to Pittsburgh to enlist, a distance of some 50 miles.

He was wounded in the hand at the battle of Liberty Gap on June 25, 1863. He fought under Sherman in Georgia, marched with Stanley after Hood, and was discharged in June 1865 following the close of the war. His rifle is still in the possession of one of his descendants. Nathaniel married Jane Hixon in 1864; she bore him two sons, Chalfant, and Norman. She died in 1868. In 1870 he married Rachel Ridenour, daughter of Jacob and Nancy Mathias Ridenour. Their children, two of whom, oddly enough, he named after Confederate leaders were: Jefferson Davis (who became a minister), Nelson, Alexander, Allen, Wade Hampton, and Mitchell King, Blanche, Laura, Kate, and Carrie King.

Nathaniel is seated in the center next to Rachel and surrounded by their family

Nat and Rachel were charter members of the Owensdale, Pennsylvania United Brethren Church where he served as an elder. He was also tax collector, school director, and road supervisor in his township for many years. He died at the age of 85 on September 30, 1923 and was followed by Rachel six weeks later. His funeral was said to have been the largest ever attended in Owensdale. A soldier escort acted as pall bearers, and 85 automobiles—one for every year of his age—were in the funeral procession. Both he and Rachel were buried in Scottdale Cemetery, Scottdale, Pennsylvania.

WILLIAM A. KING
1836 - 1908

William was the son of Julian A. King and Rebecca Cannon King. In 1840 this family were living in Lowndes County, Mississippi, where William's father died in 1848. After the death of Julian King, Rebecca moved her family to Tippah County, Mississippi. In 1860 William and his first wife, Mary were living in Chickasaw County, Mississippi, with their two daughters - Sarah Francis "Sally" and Parthema Aramitia "Mittie." After the Civil War began in April of 1861, William enlisted in the Confederate Army on June 15, 1861 at Molino, Mississippi. The Union Army at the Battle of Fort Donelson captured him on February 16, 1862. He spent several months at Camp Douglas, a Union P.O.W. camp near Chicago, Illinois, where many Confederate Soldiers froze to death. He was released in an exchange of prisoners at Vicksburg, Mississippi. William then went back into the Confederate Army after his release. During 1862 and 1863, his mother and his wife, Mary, died. His brother, Daniel, was killed at the battle of Gettysburg, in July of 1863. While on leave in March of 1864, William married Temperance Jane Reaves Corder, the widow of Eleazor Corder, a Confederate who died while a prisoner at Camp Douglas, Illinois. In June of 1864, William was wounded at New Hope Church, Georgia. According to pension records, William remained in the Confederate Army until the close of the war - April 1865.

After the war, William and Jane lived in Chickasaw County, Mississippi. They raised Jane's daughter, Virginia Elizabeth Corder, and their eight children: Henry Cannon, James Anderson, John Franklin, William Edward, Thomas Jefferson, Lucia, and twins, Rosa Belle and George Washington. By 1880, the King family had moved to Caldwell County, Texas. In 1890 they moved to Wynnewood, Indiana Territory. They came with three other families, the Mitchells, Hoopers and Welches. The Kings were farmers and worked with the Mitchells in the cotton gins around Wynnewood. William's wife, Jane, died in Wynnewood in February of 1895 and he later married Lou Ellen Cox.

In 1908, William was living in Wolfe City, Texas, when he died. His body was brought back to Wynnewood by train. His second wife Jane and two of their sons are also buried in Oaklawn Cemetery with William.

Elijah A. Kirkland
1847 -1897

Elijah was born in 1847, at Henry County, Alabama, as the third surviving child of his parents, Zacheriah and Mary Cole. He joined the Confederate States Army at the age of 17 or 18, serving in Company E, 63rd Regiment, Alabama and then Company C (Calvary), from July 1864 to the South's surrender in 1865.

On August 26, 1866 Elijah married Nancy Jane Roney, at the house of her grandfather, Hugh Roney in Henry County, Alabama, Thomas Brown Justice of the Peace performed the marriage. Nancy's father James Roney, had died five years earlier in the war.

Their son, William Warren was born in 1868, followed by Alice L., born in 1871; and Lee Roy, born in 1873. Sometime after Lee Roy's birth and 1876 the family moved to Mississippi where Mary E. was born about 1876. After Mary's birth and before 1880 the family moves to Well's Bayou Township, Lincoln County, Arkansas. In the 1880 census Elijah's occupation is enumerated as farmer. In 1897 he died at Pine Prairie, Ashley County, Arkansas after several weeks of illness.

A contemporary account of his death stated,

> *He was one of Ashley County's best citizens and most successful farmers. His death is a grievous loss not only to the neighborhood in which he resided, but to the entire County and State as well. He was in the prime of life and belonged to that valuable class of citizens who form the social and political bulwark and glory of the commonwealth. He filled the measure of usefulness and good citizenship in all the relations of life, and will be sadly mourned and missed by all who knew him. He enjoyed the highest respect, confidence and good will of his fellowmen, and the hearts of all are deeply moved with sympathy for his bereaved wife and children on whom the blow falls with such distressing weight.*

Another obituary reported: "Death of E. A. Kirkland"

> *Bro. Mitchel, his pastor, in the funeral service said 'he was above the average in his goodness,' which statement is evidently true. Dry as it was last year his farm made corn enough to do the place. He was one of the few who freely gave all he was able to the cause of Christ. Many parents desert their children when they marry, not so with this brother; his tender love, good advice and financial help ever followed them. He had two orphan children in his home and treated them as his own. He was a strong supporter of churches, schools and every good enterprise. If all church members would work as he did, every church would have its own pastor, who would be free from debt and would have both hands on the Bible. Then the pulpit would be what God intended to be, a power irresistible for doing good. A Friend.*

WILLIAM JAMES LATHAN
1840 - 1927

William James Lathan was a farmer before he enlisted in Company D, 17th Regiment, South Carolina Volunteer Infantry on January 15, 1862. He originally served under Captain James Beaty but apparently had several other company commanders due to casualties among the officer corps.

The Proceedings of the Southern Historical Society, give details of his regiment and company's involvement in several major engagements during the period of his service: Rappahannock Campaign, Malvern Hill and the Second Battle of Manassas where the Company was part of Evan's Brigade and suffered sixty-six percent casualties. His brother, Samuel Boston Lathan, known as the "Scribbler of the Family," wrote a graphic description of the battlefield and the march to Antietam, "Gleaning." Both sources show their Regiment was in the thick of the fighting at Antietam, Sharpsburg, Boonsboro, and South Mountain. His brother, Samuel was wounded and captured at the battle of South Mountain. The fighting at South Mountain was a fierce holding action to slow the Union forces as they crossed the mountains on the "Old National Highway."

During the period, December 13 through 14, 1862 William's company was in the battle of Kinston, North Carolina. Even though there is no specific mention in his records, it is safe to assume he was with his Company through all of the campaigning described so far due to the location of his outfit as mentioned in the military records. In January of 1863, he is listed, as being sick with typhoid fever and apparently did not return to his Company until October of 1863. During this illness he was in the C.S.A. General Military Hospital, No.4, in Wilmington, North Carolina and during part of this time he was on a list of those "disabled". Therefore, it seems logical that he was in the battle of Kinston due to his being put into this particular hospital. Interestingly his brother, Samuel was listed as being in this same hospital during part of the same period due to his wound at Antietam/South Mountain. It is also probable that William missed the fighting that his regiment was involved in at Jackson, Mississippi in support of the Confederate troops retreating from Vicksburg. This campaign occurred during the period of May-July of 1863 while he was sick.

Beginning, October of 1863, he was again with his Company through December of 1864 except for two short illnesses. The first time was for an illness that cannot be read from the microfilm record, but lasted only from May 16, 1864 until May 23, 1864. During this period he was again hospitalized in the C.S.A. General Military Hospital, No.4, at Wilmington. He is shown to have returned to his Company at Petersburg, Virginia on the 23 of May 1864. During the second of these illnesses he was hospitalized in the Jackson Hospital at Richmond. This second illness was listed as jaundice and lasted from October 4, 1864 until October 21, 1864. The battle of the Crater at Petersburg, Virginia occurred at the end of July 1864. Since this battle was between the two illnesses and his Company was assigned to the fort that was blown up, he should have been in the thick of it. Records at the National Archives do not contain any mention of the period between the "Crater" and the end of the war. The last entry in Sergeant William James Lathan's military record is his parole on April 10, 1865, the day after General Robert E. Lee's surrender at Appomattox.

William died April 4, 1927, fourteen days before his birthday.

John Wesley Marshall
1843 - 1904

On September 5, 1843, James Wesley Marshall was born in Greene County, Missouri. The Marshall family had lived in Green and Wright County, Missouri just prior to the Civil War. The family moved to Fort Scott, Kansas in 1861. In 1861 he was in Bourbon County, Kansas and enlisted in the Kansas 6th Regiment, Company L. His three brothers - Elias, James, and Washington Popejoy Marshall also enlisted.

Sometime between 1865 and 1870, John and his family moved to Crawford County, Kansas and by 1880 they are living in Sunset, Montague County, Texas. In 1890 he again moves with his family from Texas to Tacoma, Washington by covered wagon.

On November 13, 1904 John W. Marshall died of pneumonia in Tacoma His oldest son had died the previous February also of pneumonia. The *Tacoma News Tribune* Obituary stated:

John W. Marshall, a civil war veteran and for many years a member of Puyallup Corps, G.A.R. died at the family residence, 1327 1/2 So E St. early yesterday morning. Mr. Marshall had been a resident of Tacoma for four years. Prior to coming to this city he had resided in Puyallup, where he was widely known. He leaves a wife and a son, John G. Marshall and a daughter, Mrs. A.S. Wilkins. The funeral arrangements will be in charge of the G.A.R.

Alinus Curtis Matthews
1832 - 1914

Alinus Curtis Matthews was born February 1, 1832, Mayfield, Fulton County, New York, son of Alinus Matthews and Catherine Bovee. (Both grandfathers, Eliada Matthews and Nicholas P. Bovee fought in the Revolutionary War.) In 1834 Alinus' parents moved the family from New York to Freehold, Warren County, Pennsylvania. By the late 1850s Alinus was in Ohio for a short time and by 1860 he had moved to Knox County, Illinois where he met his future wife Jennie Taylor. Jennie was born November 7, 1842, in Upper Strasburg, Franklin County, Pennsylvania, the daughter of Samuel Taylor and Mae/Mary Stewart.

Alinus enlisted at Peoria in the Illinois 17th Infantry, Company D, under the name A. Curtis Mathews, as a corporal from Altona, Illinois. His military record indicates he was 5' 10", brown hair and blue/gray eyes. He was in 3 battles and injured twice. The first was the battle of Fredericktown, on October 21, 1862. At the battle of Donelson, February 13, 1862, he received a rifle shot to his right forearm, where the ball remained for the rest of his life. A month later on March 15, 1862, he was promoted to Second Lieutenant. The next month, between April 6 and 7, 1862, he was in the battle of Shiloh where he was again wounded, this time in the calf of his right leg and was hospitalized in Savannah and Cincinnati from April to June of 1862. On April 18, 1862, one month since his promotion to Second Lieutenant he was promoted to First Lieutenant. This promotion was most likely by vote of his Regiment for bravery, as he was also presented a sword from his hometown of Walnut Grove, Illinois. The inscription on the sword reads, "Presented to Alinus Curtis Matthews for gallantry in action in Fredericktown, Donelson, and Shiloh." This sword remains among his descendants.

The family history states that Alinus was also presented a flag which has been lost to time and so have the memories of the battle for which was presented. Alinus was medically discharged on February 18, 1863, and moved to Winona, Minnesota where he built a house for his fiancée, Jennie Taylor. That fall Jennie came by train from Walnut Grove to meet him in LaCrosse, Wisconsin. On the day of her arrival, September 30, 1863, they were married and moved to their new home in Winona, where he was a carpenter until 1873, when they moved to Minneapolis. The couple had twelve children: Harry Scott, Charles Curtis, Frank Murray, Jennie Winona, George Dunkle, Hugh Bertrand, Earnest Leslie, Grace Maud, Daisy Adele, Arthur Drake, Myrta Mae, Gertie Bell.

Alinus filed for a military pension because of the war injuries to his leg and arm and for rheumatism caused by the hardships endured in the war. In Minneapolis he worked as a millwright for Washburn-

ALINUS CURTIS MATTHEWS
1832 - 1914

Crosby now a division of Gold Medal Flour for the last 40 years of his life. Once catching his beard in the machinery and had to pull it out by the roots. (He kept it trimmed after that.) He was a member of Cataract Lodge, A. F. and died, February 14, 1914, at the age of 82 in Minneapolis and is buried at Crystal Lake Cemetery. Jennie died in Minneapolis on July 26, 1927 is also buried at Crystal Lake Cemetery.

JAMES M. MATTHEWS
1827 -1897

James M. Matthews (brother of Alinus) was born in1827, at Mayfield, Fulton County, New York. By 1860, James was living in Oasis, Waushara County, Wisconsin. On August 2, 1861 he enlisted into the Wisconsin 7th Volunteer Infantry, Company I, "The Iron Brigade" as a private, at Steven's Point. He was taken prisoner while on picket duty at Haymarket, Virginia on October 19, 1863, and held prisoner at Belle Island from October 23, 1863 until March 1864. He then rejoined the company and was discharged September 1, 1864.

On December 5, 1879, James filed for a pension, stating that while on picket duty he, Jacob Phillips, Alvin Waterman, Rufus Wilson, and two others were taken prisoner and confined to Belle Island on October 23, 1863, "Six of my company were taken prisoner. Two died in Belle Island, and after 5 months, 4 of us went back to the regiment, and after 2 1/2 months we were discharged and went home. After a short time, Rufus Wilson, one of the four, died..." In an affidavit James stated, "During the month of December I was without tent or other conveniences, and with no shoes or stockings, and that my pants were torn off nearly to the knees and no coat, that the weather was so cold that the water would freeze in my cup, and at that time I froze my feet, as stated in my application." Jacob Phillips stated, "James was a mere skeleton and scarcely able to walk when he released from prison." Due to the effects of severe frostbite James was unable work on a regular bases, winters being much worse than summers. He stated that he had redness, swelling, and open sores and that times it made it impossible for him to walk around or wear shoes. Another affidavit stated, "James is an 'Old Granny' and doctors his own feet with herbs and roots for which he was known to be the best 'Granny of the Company'." Most of his treatments were home remedies, using a salve of mutton tallow and sweet elder and a wash of blue vitriol alcohol and white lead. A previous employer learning that his injuries were from the Civil War gave James a position of whatever he could do and whenever he could do it.

James married Mrs. Margarentha Mersch Hummel. She died on December 20, 1868, just two months after the birth of their only child, Matt who was born on Oct 15, 1868. Due to James' ill health he was unable to raise the baby and his wife's family raised the child. Unfortunately, Matt never knew his father. Matt married Mayme 'Mary' Fogarty on July 15, 1903, and raised a family of seven children in the Steven's Point area.

James M. Matthews
1827 - 1897

On October 29, 1875, James married Mrs. Marietta Eliza Babcock Vrooman at Wisconsin Rapids, (then Grand Rapids) Wood County, Wisconsin. On October 4, 1889, they both entered Wisconsin's Veteran's Home (The Grand Army Home) in King, Waupaca County, Wisconsin after having been supported the last 3 years by neighbors because of declining health. James died June 6, 1897 and Maryette died July 10, 1907. They are both buried at the Wisconsin's Veteran's Home.

Alvin Greenlee McGinness
1843 - 1912

Alvin Greenlee McGinness, was born April 12, 1843 and died February 15, 1912. He was the son of William and Jane McGinness of Little Beaver Township, Lawrence County, Pennsylvania. The family originally came from Allegheny Township, Allegheny County, Pennsylvania, where William was employed as a blacksmith.

He served in Company I, 134th Pennsylvania Volunteers and was wounded at the battle of Fredericksburg, Virginia, on December 13, 1862, receiving a surgeon's discharge in April 1863.

Alvin G. McGinness married Mary Jane Hartshorn in 1866 and had a family of five children. After the war he was a farmer and died in testate, but the inventory of his property shows a lot of farm equipment and supplies, and lists several head of cattle and pigs.

Mary Jane Hartshorn

Daniel Harper McLaughlin
1845 - 1910

Daniel Harper McLaughlin was born in June of 1845 at Newville, Cumberland County, Pennsylvania, where he would reside his entire life. Before and after the war his occupation was that of a farmer. During the Civil War he served as a private in Company D, 187th Regiment Pennsylvania Volunteer Infantry.

He fought in the battles of Cold Harbor and Petersburg and was a part of the mine explosion that occured at the battle of Petersburg where Colored and White troops were slaughtered in the so-called "crater." The 187th Pennsylvania was the Guard of Honor over the remains of President Lincoln in Independence Hall, Philadelphia, and served as escort for the funeral cortege in May 1865.

He married Jane Anna Brymesser on January 25, 1877. They had six children: Roy B., Samuel H., William P., Albert L., Charles B., and Frank. He died on December 25, 1910 and is buried in the Big Spring Presbyterian Church Cemetery in Newville.

Benjamin Orbin
1836 - 1911

Benjamin Orbin, son of John Phillip Orbin, lived at Dry Hill near Broad Ford, Fayette County, Pennsylvania. He served with the 85th Regiment, Pennsylvania Volunteer Infantry during the Civil War. The granddaughter of Benjamin had his discharge papers hanging on the wall and pinned to the papers was a star from a flag that according to family tradition held that, during the battle of Kingston, North Carolina the flag was shot through and a star was hanging by a thread, Benjamin reached up and plucked the star off to save it from falling to the ground. During his service Benjamin was enlisted as a private and mustered out a sergeant.

The following are letters written by Benjamin to his father, his mother having passed away in 1854. Benjamin was 25 years old when the first letter was written:

Benjamin Orbin
1836 - 1911

Fort Good hope January the 4th, 1862.
Dear father

i take my pen to Pen you a few lines i just recieved your kind Letter wich I was Glad to hear that you ens was all well wee are all well and harty wee have Some winter here it Snowed yisterday and night before last there was a nuf to Slay if wee had eney Slays to of rodein I hav to goe about fore miles To morrow to guard a fort or help guard one co B guards fore and one bridge So wee have Something To doe it has been vary disagreeable for some Three weaks but i think it will git more pleasant This month the moast of the fighting that will Be don is expected to bee done this month if such should be the case you will hear of some Hard fighting but i say let it come the rebles will Meet a warm reception everything is quiet here on the acount of bad weather so i Cant write you a vary interesting letter so i hav to quit soon the health of the Regment is vary good at presant i was going to send some More money but i come to the conclueson that I had Better keepe some for soar shins but if wee Git pade this month I'll send some then for you to kepe for me if I come home and if I should be so onluckey to not git home you have the Best Write to it I sent you a paper or so i still git one ever day When i read them I think i might as well send Them to some of youens as to leav them lay a round we had no mail for about a weak until This evning an then there was some glat boys Some of them gat as high as seven leters so Tha had a good time reading i got a letter From uncle Thomas Stephens tha ar all well and harty Poes is all well or was Some time a goe i got a letter from a friend in Masouria tha ar giving The rebles particlar fits. Wee hav one Man in our company that went crazy Saturday Tha tooke him to town today and then had To fetch him home but tha will take him in to morow he toar some of the boys chimblys down he is from Washington County his name is parks well I'll quit for the presant hoping to hear from you soon yours with respect your Servnt Benj orbin Foley Island, SC May 29, 1863

Dear Father

I take time To pen you a few lines to let you know how wee ar giting a long wee Stil keap on this island And watch the rebs to keap them from giting possession of it every thing seams to be on a Stand Stil we don't git eney news from the north till we git mail and Then Some times not much the mail onely comes by chance Some times not for too weaks I don't think there will be enye thing don here this Somer but its hard to tel eney thing A bout what will be don but it looks to me as if there would be nothing done here of any importance for some time yet and maby not at all I Cant tell what our gun boats is doing but they keep Oup A big fus they ar Shooting nearly every night and Sometimes through the day There has been a number of boats tried to run the blackeade but i cant tell how they succeded but no doubt but what Som of them gits through wee can See them and that is all wee know A bout them onely when they Commence Shooting then wee can hear them but what success they hav wee cant tell untill wee git papers it seams like being in jail to be on this island or like Som Say jail is i never was in jail nor don't ever expect to be but if it is eney wors then this place I pitty thes Trators thay hav to be there for life let it be long or Short The Broad Ford Boys is All well and I

Benjamin Orbin
1836 - 1911

beleave they Ar all out on dress parad now I hav not been vary well for Som time but feal better this morning I think in a few days I can doe douty but I dont intend to doe deauty til I feal able Going on douty has put me backe several times and I think I will much better heare after I never like to mis douty but when one is sick it cant be helped There is talk of our Regiment being Consolidated but I don't know how soon it will be don but I expect it will be some time This Somer if it is at all if it does happen there will be sum fusing around The health of the Regiment is better now than it was last year at this time I bleave i hav nothing more to Say I Rec I Remain as ever your Son Benj Orbin I had intended to send some money but as I havent been vary well I thought it would be best to keep it til some more convenient time yours BBO Hilton Head South Carolina Feb 27, 1864

Dear Father

I take My pen in hand to pen you a few lines wee have had another fight with the gray backe on last Sunday wee Started for white Marsh Island Georga wee landed at nine Monday Morn within five miles of Savana and had a fight wright off wee had two men wounded and three taken Prissoners we Capturard 17 of thear and Returned The same day wee ar doing guard douty at hilton head now I can't say how long wee will stay here Our men is prity hard oup in Fla wee may git orders to goe thear eney moment I hope wee will git to stay here I don't like moveing The health of Our Squad is good the Broad Ford boys Is all well and in good plight The weather is warm and plesent I expect Thomas and George will be at home soon as they ar in the North I heard from uncle and aunt Stepens They wer all well I also heard from Aunt Katie Poe She is well and giting along as usial Its been some time cince I hav heard from home So I thot I would let you know how I em I hope this will find you well and injoying your self well Give all inquiring friends my Respects I hav nothing much to write so I hope you will excuse brevity — I Close now hoping Ill be sparrd to pen you a few lines soon again I remain your Son &c as ever Benj Orbin Hilton Head, SC April the 11th 1864

Dear Father

I now take time To pen you a few Lines I have nothing much to write but Ill try an pen a few lines at eney rate Wee ar Still at Hilton Head wee go on an expedition nearly evary weak be sides on guard evary other day So it keeps us buisey all the time but the time drags along vary heavy There is nothing of eney importance going on the weather is vary warm I expect wee will hav plenty of warm weather now I expect that wee will move In to Hilton Head or out on the picket line I cant tell which and maby not at all The 76 Pa has Orders to leave and the 6th Connecite [Connecticut?] So wee will hav a brisk time Guarding The health of the Troups is good there is but little Sickness here the mumps Is in our Co There is one cace of small pox in the Regiment The Small Pox is nothing like as bad as it was Some time backe wee git but little knews from home or eney place else It Seams vary lonesome not to hear from home I hav begun to think that it is no use to write but ill still pen you a few lines onct and a while The last time I heard from Uncle and Aunt Stephens they wer

Benjamin Orbin
1836 - 1911

all well Its been about two weakes cince I heard from them The last time I heard from Aunt Katie Poe she was well She would like offul well to See me and if I am Spared to git home Ill goe to see her maby you think that I wont just goe to See her a lone you mite think write but She would be part of my visit out there O she is so kind Aunt Elizabeth was well the last time I heard from her I don't hear from Uncle Jacob Rist So I cant tell you how they ar Its been a vary wet spring here I think the wet weather is about over for this Spring The Broad Ford Boys Is all well and in good plight I em well and feal well but I em giting vary Poor I j gess its the change of the weather but wee ar Run around so much that it might be the caus wee have Giv oup giting out of the army before the three years wee ust to think that the war would not last our turm but I think it will last much longer but I hope it wont Ps/" excuse this Ill composed letter Ill close Hoping that this will Reach you in good time and that you will be in good health give my respects to all inquiring friends I would like to send som Money home but I don't like to riske it by male I have sent money to Thomass wife and I hav never heard if it got through Safe It was som of Toms money that I colected that he had out when he went away Your son Benj Orbin Ill try and write Soon agane

Benjamin Orbin died in 1911.

GEORGE WALTER ORBIN
1840 - 1916

George Orbin was the younger brother of Benjamin Orbin. Before the war George was a teacher. George Walter served as a private in Company C, 85th Regiment, Pennsylvania Volunteers from October 9, 1861 until October 31, 1864. His service record included the following comment from a superior, "He is a meritorious and deserving soldier. And was in the battles of Williamsburg, and Fair Oaks, Va., and Kingston, Whitehall, and Goldsboro, N.C. He also participated in the siege and capture of Ft. Wagner S.C."

George was wounded at Morris Island, South Carolina on September 19, 1863, and contracted chronic diarrhea. He was hospitalized from January through August 1864. He rejoined his Company in September of 1864. He was mustered out in October 1864. George had two other brothers fight in the Civil War - his brother Thomas enlisted as a private in Company B, 85th Regiment of the Pennsylvania Infantry. Thomas was listed as missing-in-action on June 17, 1864, near Mire Bottom Church, Virginia. The War Department Adjutant General's Office in Washington D.C. reported on November 24, 1866, that Thomas died at Camp Lawton Prison in Georgia on November 7, 1864, of chronic diarrhea while a prisoner of war. Another brother - Joseph was drafted into the 63rd Regiment, Company F of the Pennsylvania Infantry. He suffered gunshot wounds in his leg and left arm on the 22nd of June 1864, near Petersburg, Virginia. Joseph was taken to General Hospital, Washington, D.C. where he died of his wounds and was buried in Arlington Cemetery (Grave Number 5903).

After the war George became a Methodist Minister serving numerous churches in Western Pennsylvania and died in 1916.

Aaron Parsons
1837 - 1902

Aaron Parsons was the 5th child of Daniel Hills Parsons of Enfield, Connecticut and Elizabeth Harper of Lovell, Maine. He was one of three sons that served the Union during the Civil War. His brothers - Benjamin Franklin and George Washington served from Ohio. Before the war he was a farmer, carpenter and mason. Aaron served nearly four years in the Civil War with the 4th West Virginia and his campaigns included: Chattanooga, Vicksburg, and Youngs Point, Louisiana.. After his discharge form the service he married Mary Malissa Jones. It is interesting to note that the three brothers: Aaron, Benjamin, and George Parsons all married women from the same family. Aaron married Mary Malissa Jones, George Washington married Lavinia Jones and Benjamin Franklin Parsons married their mother Charlotta McKnight Jones. Aaron was the administrator of the estate of Charlotta's first husband Wesley Jones in 1860.

He took Sarah Ellen Barnhart of West Virginia as his second wife on October 2, 1871 at Syracuse, New York. Sarah was born March 27, 1852 at Virginia and died January 30, 1918 at Brady, Lincoln County, Nebraska. The following is his obituary:

Born October 1st 1837. Aaron Parsons was born near Chester, Meigs County, Ohio in the year 1837. Died near Stebbardsville, Ohio, April 22, 1902 at the age of 65 years 6 months and 22 days. He served his country nearly four years in the civil war and his comrades, several of whom are today present, bear witness that he was a bold, faithful and loyal soldier. In his dealings with his fellowmen he was strictly honest and a good citizen. At the close of the war he was married to Melisia Jones, who preceded him to the spirit world. To this union were born three children, one son and two daughters. He was again married to Sarah E. Barnhart and to this marriage was born six children. Four sons and two daughters. All of them are present today except two sons who are in Nebraska, One of which [this is Christian E. per Dorothy L. Parker] came here to see his father and returned only a few days before his death. He united with the Christian church near Chester in 1875. After moving to Dowington he removed his membership to the free will Baptist church of that place. He has always lived a consistent Christian life. Having to some extent lost the blessing of hearing and being in feeble health for some years he did not attend public worship as he did in his earlier life. A few minutes after being stricken in his last illness he said "My time has come. I am ready to go" and a few days later he had a blessed experience when he said "He was Happy that the Lord heard and answered his prayers and he asked his family to meet him in Heaven."

John Purdy
1833-1926

John Purdy was born at Allegheny County, Pennsylvania in 1833, the son of Farmer Purdy and Esther Richmond of Frankfort Springs, Hanover Township, Pennsylvania. John was raised on his parents' farm.

He served with Company H, 140th Regiment, Pennsylvania Volunteers during the Civil War. He saw action in many battles and was twice wounded - at Gettysburg and Spotsylvania. He served with Colonel Richard P. Roberts (1820-1863) and Sargeant David Walker Scott (1830-1911) who also served in the 140th Pennsylvania Volunteers Regiment from its inception in August 1862. They were all three residents of Beaver County, Pennsylvania, and each paid the cost of war during the battle of the Wheatfield at Gettysburg on July 2, 1863. Purdy received a minor bullet wound in the foot, Scott suffered a much more serious wound by taking a bullet through the mouth, and their commanding officer, Colonel. Roberts paid the supreme sacrifice, the lost of his life.

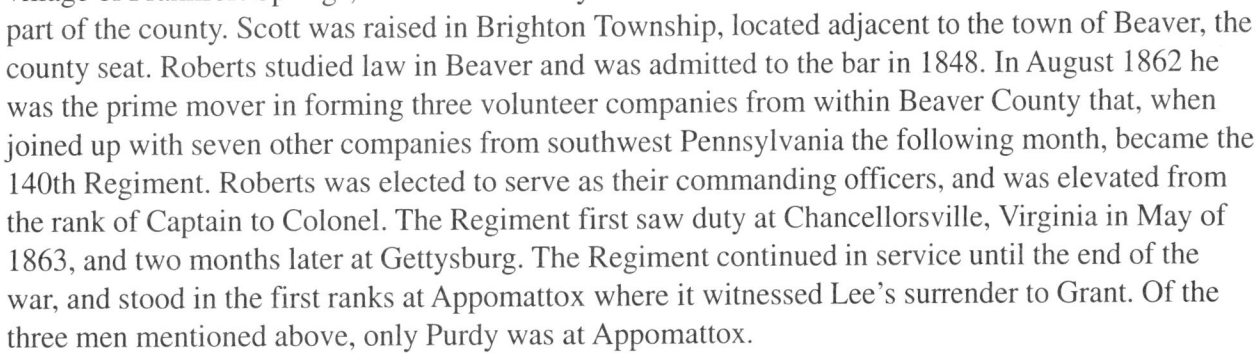

Roberts and Purdy grew up as neighbors in the small village of Frankfort Springs, located in the very southern part of the county. Scott was raised in Brighton Township, located adjacent to the town of Beaver, the county seat. Roberts studied law in Beaver and was admitted to the bar in 1848. In August 1862 he was the prime mover in forming three volunteer companies from within Beaver County that, when joined up with seven other companies from southwest Pennsylvania the following month, became the 140th Regiment. Roberts was elected to serve as their commanding officers, and was elevated from the rank of Captain to Colonel. The Regiment first saw duty at Chancellorsville, Virginia in May of 1863, and two months later at Gettysburg. The Regiment continued in service until the end of the war, and stood in the first ranks at Appomattox where it witnessed Lee's surrender to Grant. Of the three men mentioned above, only Purdy was at Appomattox.

Richard Roberts was married and had a daughter, Emma, who was eight years of age when her father marched off to war in 1862. Roberts's wife died the year before, leaving Emma to the care of relatives and friends. From the day that he left for the service, until the day before he was killed, Roberts wrote to his daughter almost on a daily basis. On July 2, 1863, riding at the head of his Regiment, Richard Roberts took a bullet to the chest and died almost instantly. His body, having been stripped of his uniform and dress sword presented to him by the citizens of Beaver, was recovered by his troops several days later and was returned home for burial along side of his wife in the Beaver Cemetery. A year later, following the battle of the Wilderness, his sword was recovered from a dead confederate officer and sent back to Beaver County, where it was presented to his orphaned daughter, Emma Roberts.

In 1868, John Purdy married Hannah Christy. They first made their home in Brighton Township and later in the village of New Sheffield, Hopewell Township where he died in 1926.

WILLIAM RAY RIDDLE
1830 - 1879

William Ray Riddle was born January 28, 1830. He was the son of William and Eve Mogle Riddle. William first married Margaret Catherine Riddle, a first cousin, and second Lavina Titterington.

William served in the Civil War in the 206th Pennsylvania Volunteer Infantry, Company C. This unit was at the defense of the Bermuda Hundred and was in the trenches at Petersburg. William died of complications from the war on August 9, 1879 and is buried at Shiloh Cemetery in Decker's Point.

Lavina Titterington Riddle

Their son, William Horace wss born April 9, 1865 he died on July 21, 1886 when his foot was entangled in the horses stirrup. He was laid to rest with his father.

William Horace Riddle

Aaron Shoemaker Ridenour
1844 - 1914

Aaron Shoemaker Ridenour was born near what is now Scottdale, Pennsylvania, on March 2, 1844, the son of Jacob and Nancy Mathias Ridenour. As a young child he was playing at the table with his sister when she accidentally stabbed him in the left eye with a pair of scissors, leaving him blind in one eye. As a young man he learned the cooper's trade (barrel making) and was employed in that capacity at the Overholt Distillery near his home.

Aaron - 1863

On July 2, 1863, with the cannons of Gettysburg audible in the distance (according to the diary of a local resident), nineteen year-old Aaron answered Governor Curtin's urgent plea for volunteers to meet the emergency created by Lee's invasion of the Commonwealth. Aaron enlisted in Company G, 54th Regiment, Pennsylvania Volunteer Infantry, a three-month's "home guard" regiment. They were sent not to Gettysburg, but to Ohio, where another rebel force, under the command of the infamous John Hunt Morgan and his "Raiders" had invaded Northern soil, wreaking havoc and destruction, while evading capture, since crossing the Ohio River into Indiana.

The 54th and 57th Regiments, under the command of General J.H. Brooks, were first ordered to Pittsburgh to await equipment. They were then sent down the Ohio to Wheeling; from where, provided with mounts, they were deployed to intercept Morgan. They succeeded in cutting him off near Salineville, Ohio, where a skirmish was fought resulting in Morgan's surrender. The crisis having passed, the Regiment was mustered out at Pittsburgh on August 17. As one historian observed, "It is to the credit of these troops that, though not required to do so, they went out of the state willingly when the success of the expedition and its speedy termination seemed to require it."

In 1866, at the age of 22, Aaron converted to Christ at the Walnut Hill United Brethren Church near Scottdale. It was probably a result of his conversion that he changed his occupation, employment in a distillery being incompatible with the strict temperance position of the United Brethren. In the years following his conversion he worked at various occupations, including peddler, butcher, and sawyer. On November 4, 1869 he married Elizabeth Stauffer, daughter of John M. and Katrina Sherrick Stauffer. The

Aaron and his best friend John Mauk

Aaron Shoemaker Ridenour
1844 - 1914

Stauffers, like the Overholts, were Mennonite farmers and distillers whose descendants later made their fortunes in the coal and coke industry. Aaron and Elizabeth became the parents of nine children: Jennie S., Chess B., Addie S., Homer S., Nettie S., Edith S., Lester S., Clark L., and Pearl M. Ridenour. They resided in the vicinity of Scottdale until 1885 when they removed to Lecompton, Douglas County, Kansas. They remained in Kansas until 1891 when Elizabeth's failing health required them to return to Pennsylvania. By 1894 they were residing on the old Davidson farm on the Narrows Road, about a mile north of Connellsville. There they lived until 1911 when they removed to near Warren, Ohio. Aaron died September 5, 1914 at the age of 70 and was survived by Elizabeth, who died July 10, 1932 at the age of 83. They are both buried in Oakwood Cemetery, Warren, Ohio.

Their grandson William Aaron Yocum (1907-1996) related the following story about Aaron in his memoirs which gives a glimpse of his character:

Grandfather Ridenour was a godly man, honest to the core. He grew vegetables and peddled them in a one horse wagon. It is told that one customer ran a bill and did not pay. Every time he passed the man on the street he was courteous to him. Finally, he stopped Grandfather on the street and asked, "Why do you always speak to me, though I have done wrong to you?"Grandfather said, "Because you are my friend." The man finally paid the whole debt.

David Ridenour
1841 - 1901

David E. Ridenour was born in 1841 near what is now Scottdale, Pennsylvania, and moved with his family to Illinois when he was about 10 years of age. During the Civil War David joined the 112th Illinois Volunteer Infantry, Company D. After the war he married Mary J. Payton on February 15, 1866. They made their home in Henry County, Illinois but later moved to Page County, Iowa where David died of cancer sometime after 1901.

GEORGE W. RIDENOUR
1835 - 1902

George W. Ridenour was born November 3, 1835 near what is now Scottdale, Pennsylvania. On February 25, 1860, he married Priscilla Booher, who bore him eight children: John, Doritha Mae, Edwin, Cora Bell, Harry O., Walter, Guy, and Reid T. Ridenour.

During the Civil War he served in Company F (later B), 168th Pennsylvania. After the war he worked as a sawyer and lumber merchant, but in later years was granted a pension due to paralysis and other ill effects caused by the explosion of a shell which injured him during the war.

George and his family lived near Scottdale, but moved to Fairchance, Pennsylvania. He died at McKeesport, Pennyslvania on August 25, 1902. Pearl M. Ridenour (1892-1974), his niece, related that he had been caring for his son in his home at McKeesport, and when he stepped out of the house he fell over dead. His widow, "Aunt Priss" as she was called, died in 1926. They are buried in the Scottdale Cemetery.

JOHN B. RIDENOUR
1833 - 1891

John B. Ridenour was born in Westmoreland County, Pennsylvania, on May 2, 1833, the son of John and Susanna Bechtel Ridenour, the second of twelve children. Tragedy visited the family in 1850 when two of his brothers and a sister died, probably in the great cholera epidemic that swept the nation. The next year the family removed to Illinois, settling first in Fulton County, then two years later, in Henry County, near Woodhull. Young John attended school until the age of 22. That he was skillful with his pen is evident from his letters that are preserved, as well as from a poem that he composed for his mother while serving in the Union Army. In 1859 he married Lois Payton, a native of Indiana, who bore him three children: William H., Mary E., and Elton A. Ridenour.

During the Civil War he enlisted in Company A, 55th Illinois Volunteer Infantry. He took part in the battle of Shiloh on April 6, 1862 where he was severely wounded and was sent home to recover. After 60 days he rejoined his Regiment at Moscow, Tennessee. He participated in a three-day battle at Chickasaw Bayou, as well as the capture of Arkansas Post in the Winter of 1862-1863. He worked on the famous Grant Canal, and participated in the battle of Champion Hill, and the long siege of Vicksburg. He then went on to

John B. Ridenour
1833 - 1891

Jackson, Mississippi and took part in the siege of that city. From there he returned to Vicksburg and up the Mississippi to Memphis with Sherman's Army. He fought in a skirmish at Tuscumbia in October 1863 and took part in the battle of Missionary Ridge the next month. He remained with Sherman's Army until mustered out on June 2, 1864. He then promptly re-enlisted and was engaged in the battles at Kennesaw Mountain, east of Atlanta, and Ezra Chapel. He took part in the siege of Atlanta and the battle of Gainesboro, all in the summer of 1864. He then marched with Sherman 300 miles through Georgia and Alabama in pursuit of Hood. Upon returning to Atlanta he again marched with Sherman to Savannah and participated in the capture of Fort McAllister.

He then accompanied Sherman on his famous march from Savannah, and took part in the battles of Columbia, South Carolina and Bentonville, North Carolina, before finally moving on to Washington at the close of the war. In all he was under enemy fire 120 days. By the time of his discharge, on June 15, 1865 he had risen from the rank of private to that of captain. He was elected Lt. Colonel, but never received the commission because of the end of the war.

After the war he was became a lumber merchant in Woodhull, Iillinois, and was a respected citizen of his community. In religion, he was a Methodist, and in politics, a Republican. He remarked in one of his letters regarding the election of 1884: "I am a Prohibition Teetotaler, but I shall vote for Blaine and Logan. I fought under Logan four years in the army and I know him like a book and love him as a brother." John B. Ridenour died December 18, 1892, according to his family Bible [a gift from his men after the war]. He drowned in the water, in the pit under the scales at his lumberyard. Apparently he was either checking some stock stored under the scale and slipped and fell in, or some boards broke and he fell through. His wife found him; when he was late coming home, she went to look for him. People have said that she never could get over how he went through the Civil War in comparatively safety (he was wounded at Shiloh and came home in time for his daughter's birth, but later returned to duty) only to drown a short distance from home."

WILLIAM W. RIDENOUR
1841 - 1908

William W. Ridenour was born December 7, 1841 in Greene County, Pennsylvania, the son of Jacob and Nancy Mathias Ridenour. As a young man William traveled west to Streator, Illinois and enlisted in the 129th Illinois Volunteer Infantry, Company A. He was with Sherman on his famous "March to the Sea," and his daughter Sadie Ridenour Lozier (1877-1980) recalled her father saying that the troops moved so rapidly on that march that they slept on the bare ground and would awake with their hair frozen fast to the earth. She also recalled that the name of Sherman was always held in high regard in the Ridenour home.

On October 14, 1867, he married Elizabeth Yothers, daughter of Bishop Henry Yothers, an itinerant Mennonite preacher. She bore him six children: Aaron W., Franklin W., Martin M., Della Mae, Sadie L., and Charles D. Ridenour. They made their home near Streator until 1871 when their house was destroyed by a tornado.

William was on the back porch when he saw it approaching and quickly gathered his wife and children into the yard where they clung to a fence post and watched as the twister struck the house. They lost everything but a clock. After this they returned to Pennsylvania and settled near Scottdale. Later they removed to New Stanton, where William helped build the New Stanton Coke Ovens. He died on October 15, 1908 and is buried in the Seanor Cemetery, New Stanton.

SAMUEL RISHEL
1829-1909

While working on the Hein Baugh farm, near Gibbon Glade, Pennsylvania an army recruiter came around looking for men to sign up to fight. Samuel signed up even though he had a wife and several children at home. Although, a Fayette County history book has him serving with the 17th Pennsylvania Infantry Company (also known as the 162nd Pennsylvania Volunteers) after close inspection of his discharge papers it appears he fought with the 17th West Virginia. The 17th West Virginia was organized in Wheeling, West Virginia. Samuel was attached to the Reserve Division of Harpers Ferry west of Sleepy Hollow from September 27, 1864 to March of 1865; and then he was attached to the First Brigade 1st Infantry Division until June 30, 1865.

His service involved moving into Clarksburg, West Virginia guarding railroad and doing garrison duty until he was mustered out June 30th 1865. The 17th West Virginia spent most of its service on sealing off Harpers Ferry and surrounding environs from Confederates. The 17th West Virginia suffered one killed in action and twenty-four from disease.

In 1874, Samuel and his wife Catherine purchased a farm from Andrew Chidester with a land warrant that was equivalent to a government loan - the land consisted of 147 ½ acres and the farm still remains in the family. Samuel died on the farm, April 28, 1909, and his wife Catharine died 26 days later on April 28. They lie in the Old Salem Cemetery very close to where they lived. The photo above of Samuel in his uniform is a charcoal rendition done by W.E. Kelly, probably from a contemporary photograph.

Samuel Rishel and Family

DAVID WALKER SCOTT
1830 - 1911

David Walker Scott was born in Brighton Township, Beaver County, Pennsylvania in 1830. In August of the second year of the war, David and scores of other Beaver County residents volunteered in the service of their country. They joined the 140th Pennsylvania and three Companies were formed F, H and I. The volunteers from Brighton Township were assigned to Company I. On the early morning of September 3rd the three companies of volunteers marched down Third Street to the cheers of many of its citizens who came out to bid them good-bye. The men arrived at Camp Curtain in Harrisburg where they joined the rest of the 140th. On January 14, 1863 at Falmouth the Army of the Potomac's winter headquarters David was promoted to Second Sergeant retroactive to the date of enlistment on April 20, 1863. He was again promoted to First Sergeant of Company I.

The 140th saw its first action at the battle of Chancellorsville in Virginia they went into action again two months later, on July 2nd at a small crossroads town called Gettysburg in Pennsylvania. The Regiment distinguished itself that day in the struggle that has gone down in history as the "battle of the Wheatfield." David Scott was wounded at the fight and this is a letter David wrote to his Mother:

July 6th 1863
Dear mother,

Knowing your anxiety to here from me since the battle, I concluded to writ a few lines, although I am not able to give you particulars. I received my wound on the 3rd (actually the second), the same day that col. (Roberts) was killed. I thought it was all up to me. There was two of our company taken prisoner attempting to get me off the field, B.F. Welsh and Wm Agnew. It was about dusk. The rebs got everything I had but my pocket book and bible. When Benj. Welsh left me I gave them to him. I had $24 in my pocket book. When he left me I thought my time had come to an end. I could neither speak nor swallow, and my wound was bleeding most profusely. About 8 o'clock that night I began to feel some better, and go and see if I could find some water, when there was a reb come up to me and asked what I had wanted. He then took my canteen and poured the water out of his into mine. He then showed me a house a few roads farther back, told me to fall back to it if I was able, and then they would take great care of me. I got to the house and found the rebs in large quantity. They were using it for a hospital. I got one of the rebels to cut my beard off. They all seemed very friendly and tried to do everything they could to make me comfortable. I stayed very close to the pump, and used cold water on my wound. The next eve our forces drove the rebs back, and I got back to my our own lines. I hadn't any water for 2 days and nights, but that was enough for I couldn't swallow anything else. The ball entered under the left jaw about an inch from the right of my left ear, and came out at the other side, knocking out 4 teeth and fracturing my jaw. The doctor said it was a very sore wound,

DAVID WALKER SCOTT
1830 - 1911

but not dangerous. I got my beard all shaved off. Our regiment lost very heavy T. (Thomas) Hunter came off safe. John stoker has one arm off. Our hospital tents are about 2 miles from Gettysburg. I don't feel able to write anymore at present. I have had no word from home for about a month as it is about that long since we got mail. It might be that I would be home for awhile at_____ I am not going to soldier much more. I will try playing off awhile too. Don't give yourselves any unnecessary trouble about me, I will get along somehow. I borrowed $15 dollars since I came to the hospital, and that will do me until I get my pocket book back from Benj. Welsh.

Yours
David W. Scott

After a period of recuperation in the 1st Division Hospital in Gettysburg, he went home on extended leave, and was discharged at Pittsburgh on surgeons certificate, dated February 20, 1865. David's Mother died on September 11, 1864 at the age of 64 a little more than three months after his military discharge. David married Caroline Barclay of Brighton Township on June 1, 1865. Following the death of his father, William Scott, on November 27, 1866, David inherited the family homestead. David Scott died in 1911 and is buried along with his family in the Beaver Cemetery.

David Walker Scott and family

Survivors of the 140th Pa. Vol. Assembled at Reunion at the Residence of J.B. Johnson, Canonsburg PA. Sept. 12 1911

WILLIAM SMITH TERRY
1830 - 1895

William Smith Terry was born in Laurens County, South Carolina in 1830. His father, John McDowell Terry was born in 1795 in South Carolina and his mother Mary Octavia Jones was born in 1800.

William probably first served in the 19th South Carolina Infantry. He was a private. He seems to also have served in the Arkansas Confederate Army, Company A, 10th Regiment. William's two brothers - Wesley and Robert also fought in the war. Mary Norfleet states, "Billie, Wesley and Robert all served as Confederate soldiers and were captured and imprisoned. Robert was captured at the Battle of Helena, July 4, 1863 and was imprisoned first at Alton, Illinois and later at Fort Delaware." Elcybeth Vance says, "Uncle "Billie" was so starved that his wife put all food under lock and key and allowed it to him by small amounts until he could take a normal meal. He would have died if allowed to eat to the full after such long starvation."

About 1866, Wiliam and his wife, Elizabeth and their family move to Ashley County, Arkansas where he operated a saw and grist mill with his brother, Robert Y. H. Terry. There was a brief mention of him in an 1867 Arkansas newspaper, "W. S. Terry put a forty horse power engine and improved machinery at his sawmill six miles south of Hamburg." However, he may have returned to South Carolina briefly as his last child, Sallie, is born there in 1871.

William died on August 13, 1895 of typhoid-malarial fever in Carter Township, Ashley County, Arkansas.

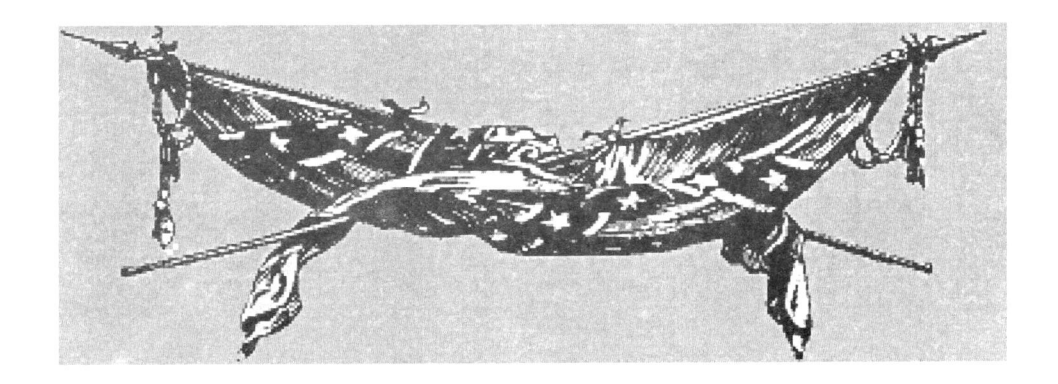

John L. Thompson
1845 - 1918

John L. Thompson was the son of David and Elizabeth Love Thompson. He served in the Civil War as a private in Captain Cook's Company G, 78th Regiment. He married Josephine Reynolds. John L. Thompson died in February 1918 and is buried in Oak Park Cemetery in New Castle.

His obituary appeared in the *New Castle News*:

The death of John L. Thompson, aged 72 years, occurred Saturday night at the family home, 563 East Long Avenue, following a long illness. He was born in Pulaski Township and was a son of David and Elizabeth Love Thompson, old residents of that place. He was a member of the G.A.R. and was a Civil War veteran, being a private in Captain Cook's Company, Co. G, 78th regiment. He was widely and favorably known and the news of his death will cause sorrow to a large circle of friends. He is survived by his widow and the following children, Mrs. F.A. Crowe of Cambridge Springs, Mrs. A.C. Patterson of Brownsville, H.J. Thompson, C.R, Thompson, Mrs. R.E. Francis and Miss Florence Thompson of this city. Two brothers and two sisters, J.H. Thompson, Plumber Thompson, Mrs. W.R. Hays and Mrs. Adeline Thompson all of Wilmington Township, also survive. Interment was made In the Oak Park Cemetery.

Josephine Thompson

ABRAHAM LOREN VANEPS
1834 - 1908

Abraham and Amanda Vaneps

Abraham Loren Vaneps was born in 1834. He married first, Nancy Jane McCormick and second, Amanda Jones Crippen.

Abraham enlisted on August 13, 1862, in Company F, 145th Pennsylvania, commanded by Captain Kimball Stiles. He was treated at Lincoln and Palmer Hospitals while in the service. A letter in his pension file written by his Lieutenant, Stephen H. Evans, in 1895, stating that after the battle of Fredericksburg in December 1862, Abraham was standing guard at Brigade Headquarters under a severe storm of rain and sleet and when he returned to the Regiment the next day he could not speak and was in the hospital until just before the battle of Chancellorsville. He was mustered out May 31, 1865 at Alexandria, Virginia.

Abraham had two brothers who also fought in the Civil War - William served with the 2nd Berdan's Sharpshooters; and Hiram - who served with the 145th Company F, died during the war of disease.

Abraham died on September 4, 1908. He was buried Sutton Hill Cemetery, Deerfield Township, Warren County Pennsylvania.

John Wareham
1830 - 1890

John Wareham was born September 3, 1831. He married Nancy McKinley Phipps in 1854.

John fought with the 4th Pennsylvania Calvary, Company K., organized at Harrisburg, Philadelphia and Pittsburgh between August and October before being sent to Washington D.C. The 4th Pennsylvania Calvary fought in almost all the battles of the Army of the Potomac its battle honors include: Yorktown, the Seven Days battles, Harrison's landing South Mountain, Antietam, Shepherdstown, Fredericksburg, and the "Mud March." John participated in these battles before being discharged by surgeons certificate on January 27, 1863. He did re-enlist with the 107th Pennsylvania Volunteers.

John's brother George fought with the 4th Pennsylvania. He and Isaac Hillkirk's grandchild married making them grandfathers-in-law. John who was also known as "Big John" died in 1890.

Jesse Wheeler
1837 - 1914

Jesse Wheeler was born March 16, 1837 in Johnston County, North Carolina, the fifth of nine children of Jesse and Lurany Johnson Wheeler. Early in his life Jesse knew that he wanted to be a minister and tried to prepare himself for that profession. In 1855 he enrolled in the Ministerial School at Wake Forest College. The year 1857 was an eventful year for Jesse Wheeler. On July 2nd he married Catherine Johnson and in October at the Cape Fear Conference in Wake County he was ordained as a minister and his name was placed on the Roll of Ministers. By 1859, Catherine and Jesse had two children: Sarah and Charles. Jesse had been the minister for several churches in the area while continuing his studies at Wake Forest College. In September 1861 the War had cast its shadow over the South and Jesse felt that he must do his part. Leaving Catherine and the children with Johnson relatives, he enlisted at Auburn, North Carolina, on September 18, 1861, first for one year and later "for the War."

Surprisingly, he did not enlist as a Chaplain. He wanted to be a soldier and he was proud of going in as private Third Corp, Company D, 31st Regiment, North Carolina Infantry. On December 20, 1862, Jesse Wheeler's name was listed on the *Roll of Honor* in his Regiment. By April 1863 he was stationed at Fort Sumter. On May 31, 1864, Jesse Wheeler was taken prisoner at Cold Harbor, Virginia and was imprisoned at Fort

Jesse Wheeler
1837 - 1914

Lookout, Maryland. On July 12, he was transferred to the prison at Elmira, New York, where he remained until the end of the war. Prison records at Elmira indicate that Jesse Wheeler was a Minister of the Gospel and conducted religious services at the prison. On May 19, 1865, he subscribed to the *Oath of Allegiance* and was allowed to return to his home in North Carolina.

Upon his return home he learned that Catherine and the children had died in 1862. After a few months Jesse went back to Wake Forest College to finish the work that he left in 1861. On January 10, 1870, Jesse Wheeler and Susanna Watkins Rogers (a war widow) were married at the home of her parents, Newbern Robert and Nancy Watkins at Rolesville, North Carolina. Jesse and Susanna had nine children but only six lived to adulthood. After serving as minister to churches in Union and Rockingham Counties in North Carolina, Jesse and Susanna decided to move west to Indian Territory so that Jesse could use his training in Missionary Work. Three of their sons were born in North Carolina: Robert, Jr., Walter R., and James E. One son, Jesse Y. was born in Arkansas and Frank J. and daughter Mary were born in Indian Territory (later Oklahoma).

In 1896 the family settled in Atoka, Indian Territory, where Jesse was a circuit riding minister preaching to Native Americans and early settlers and any who would listen. He learned the Choctaw Indian language and could speak it fluently. It was not unusual for Federal Marshals to spend the night at Jesse Wheeler's house when they were taking prisoners to the jail at Muskogee, sleeping on the floor handcuffed to their prisoners. In 1900, Jesse Wheeler moved his family to Wynnewood in Garvin County where his sons established themselves in business and professional life and daughter Mary became a teacher.

He was awarded the Southern Cross of Honor in 1904. Jesse died from cancer on March 28, 1914 in Wynnewood, Oklahoma and is buried at Oaklawn Cemetery. Susanna died during an influenza epidemic in 1910 and is also buried in Wynnewood's Oaklawn Cemetery.

CREDITS

CREDITS

All photographs and family information are used with permission of the families of the men profiled and may not be reproduced in writing or electronic format without written consent of the owner.

Adronian Armagost - Dr. Harry Sharp
Benjamin Baxter - Linda Currie
Truman Beard - William Huber
George Blackburn – Steve Blackburn
Theopholis Bonzo - David White
Daniel Brobst - Arthur Holmes III
Emmet Brockway - Arthur Holmes III
Thomas Bolton Burns - Linda Walls
Adam Clark – Esther McDermott
Hiram Consla – Robert Thickman
Josiah Coulter - Chuck Coulter
Alexander Craig - David J. Huffman
Wilson Dean - Brent Morgan
John Fay - Dan & Annette Fay
Richard Gardner – Elizabeth Grandey
Reuben George - Teri Merchant
Joseph Groff - Alice Luckhardt
William Harpst - Dan & Annette Fay
John Hardenbrook- Elaine Swan
William Hardenbrook - Elaine Swan
Martin Harry - Timothy Adams
Milton Hepler - Linda Walls
Thomas Hepler - Linda Walls
Jacob Hess - Arlene Baker
A.F. Hill - Scot Novak
Issac Hillkirk – Lynn Schneider
Issac Hillkirk - sketch by Martin Ghegan
Rev. Nicholas Holmes - Janet Cornell
William Huffman - David J. Huffman
Joseph Jackson – Martha Henriod
Benjamin Johnson – Morris Johnson
Daniel Jones - Dr. Harry Sharp
Jesse Jones - Scot Novak

Jesse G. Jones - transcribed by Marlene Grubb for publication in the *Southwestern Journal* of Knoxville County, Texas between 1911-1912. (Microfilm record in the Archives of the University of Texas, Austin, TX); photograph - Cheryl Grubb Christenson

John Kane – information based on a story by Lee Walter, written in 1900, and photograph – Linda Squires

CREDITS

Morgan Kefover - Scot Novak
Nathaniel King - Tom Ridenour
William King – Michael Grissom and the Wynnewood, Oaklawn Cemetery
Elijah Kirkland - Elroy Christenson
William Lathan - Bill Lathan
John Marshall - Cheryl Grubb Christenson
Alinus Matthews - Linda Currie
James Matthews - Linda Currie
Alvin McGinness - Jean Platt
Daniel Harper McLaughlin - Tom Ridenour
Benjamin Orbin - David Orbin & Tom Ridenour
George Orbin - David Orbin & Tom Ridenour
Aaron Parsons - Don Parsons
John Purdy - Richard Temple
William Riddle – Dorothy Smeyers
Aaron Ridenour - Tom Ridenour
David Ridenour - Tom Ridenour
George Ridenour - Tom Ridenour
John Ridenour - Tom Ridenour
William Ridenour - Tom Ridenour
Samuel Rishel - Larry Rishel
David Scott - Richard Temple
Wm. F. Terry - Elroy Christenson
John Thompson - Bea Mansfield
Abraham Vaneps - James Hunter
John Wareham – Lynn Schneider
Jesse Wheeler – Michael Grissom and the Wynnewood, Oaklawn Cemetery

Regimental histories provided by the National Park Service - *Soldiers and Sailors* System.
Most of these veterans have been found at familyoldtimephotos.com
Samuel P. Bates. *Pennsylvania Volunteers*. Published, 1870.

Front cover illustration - Matthew T. Fox, Sr.
Back cover photograph - Thomas L. Hollowak

APPENDIX

APPENDIX

For Civil War Soldier Pension & Military Records:

The National Archives:
In person:
Archives I
7th Street and Pennsylvania Avenue, Washington, D.C.

By mail:
Archives II – College Park, Maryland
Archives Library Information Center (NWCCA)
Room 2380, - 8601 Aldephi Road
College Park, MD 20740-6001

The Horse Soldier – Research Service for Soldiers
3506 Majestic Pine Lane
Fairfax, VA 22033
Attention – Vonnie S. Zullo
www.horsesoldier.com

APPENDIX

To preserve Civil War Landmarks and battlefields please consider a donation to the following:

The Civil War Preservation Trust
1331 H Street, N.W. – Suite 1001
Washington, D.C. 20005

Friends of the National Parks at Gettysburg
P.O. Box 4622
Gettysburg, PA 17325

National Park Foundation
11 Dupont Circle, N.W. – Suite 600
Washington, D.C. 20036 [attention – M. Holland]

The Conservation Fund
1800 North Kent Street, Suite 1120
Arlington, VA 22209

Central Maryland Heritage League
200 W. Main Street
P.O. Box 721
Middletown, MD 21769

Central Virginia Battlefields Trust
604-A William Street, Suite 1
Fredericksburg, VA 22401

Save the Franklin Battlefield
P.O. Box 851
Franklin, TN 37065

Cedar Creek Battlefield Foundation
P.O. Box 229
Middletown, VA 22645

Wynnewood Confederate Monument Contribution
Museum of Southern History
P.O. Box 215
Wynnewood, OK 73098

The Museum of the Confederacy
The Annual Fund
1201 East Clay Street
Richmond, VA 23219